Marlissa,
It is great to
be able to work v
you! Casey

MW00723957

LORD OF **ALL**

Lord of All
Editor Casey Veatch

ISBN: 978-0-9817061-5-3
Library of Congress Control Number: 2015950845

Cover design: Jason VanDorsten www.jasonvandorsten.com
Layout design: Jen Anderson of www.HisandHerAnderson.com

Believe Books publishes the inspirational life stories of extraordinary Christians from around the world. Requests for information should be addressed to: **Believe Books** at www.believebooks.com

Printed in the United States of America

EMBRACING UNITY & ETERNITY THROUGH JESUS CHRIST
IN NORTHERN VIRGINIA & BEYOND

LORD OF ALL

CASEY VEATCH
EDITOR

BELIEVE BOOKS
Life Stories That Inspire
WASHINGTON, DC

TABLE OF CONTENTS

ACKNOWLEDGEMENTS

When any project is completed and it involves multiple individuals, it is always dangerous to start naming people because you will leave someone out and hear about it later. I am very grateful for the many souls who helped this book come to fruition. I will limit these acknowledgements to my family and those directly involved with this book. If I leave someone out, I pray that you will remember the main point of our Lord's message…grace. ;)

It all starts with gratitude to God for giving all of us the opportunity to share His message through this book. I thank my wife, Lisa, for being the final person God used to get it through my head that eternity is all about the work Jesus did for us, not my "good works." I thank my kids Cal, Courtney, Bennet and Ainsley who teach me daily about gratitude, humility and love. Thanks to Mike Minter for taking time out of his extremely demanding schedule to be our content editor and for being a faithful teacher of God's word for over 40 years. I have benefitted greatly from his teaching. Our fearless publisher, Dianne Haskett, who certainly walked by faith through this project, has been an invaluable partner in what we hope is the first of multiple projects. God gave us the perfect publisher. Thanks to Rick Groux for introducing us to Dianne. Thanks to all of our writers who share the same passion of proclaiming Jesus and, through Him, bringing reconciliation and healing to all people; to Jason VanDorsten for using his creative talents for our captivating cover design; and to Jen Anderson for her polished interior layout.

Thanks to Bruce and Diana Campbell for their wisdom and friendship; to Jerry Leachman for his spiritual coaching and encouragement; to Vaneetha Rendall, Brian Jackson, George Light and Carl Grant for their loyalty and inspiration; to our prayer team: Alex Marcus, Paul Farrell, Lynne Farrell, Todd Bramblett, Bob Maistros, Michelle Hoffman, John Endlich, Fred Leamnson, Rick Thomas, Kishore Carey and Robert Brandau. God answered your prayers for our writers, editors and families. Thanks to Jack Quarles, Brian Jackson, John Endlich, Mike Meyers, Bill Hurley, Gavin Long and Lee Self for helping me identify writers.

Finally, we thank you for reading this book and hope that you, too, will see Jesus for who He is and that you will see all people the way God sees them.

INTRODUCTION
By Casey Veatch

I am not a pastor and I do not have a theological degree. I am simply a businessperson who has worked in Northern Virginia my entire career. For some time, I have felt inspired to assemble this book – written by a diverse group of people from Northern Virginia who each proclaim Jesus as their Savior and Lord – as a testimony to the fact that He is, indeed, Lord of All. As different as each of these stories may be, the common thread among them shows our common love of Jesus and faith in His saving grace.

I have always enjoyed and appreciated the broad diversity of people in our community, and I have wanted to find a way to encourage greater unity both inside and outside the church. It occurred to me that if we were to know the personal stories of men and women of God who serve among us, it might help draw us all together in Christian love.

My own story includes an atheist and a Muslim who surprisingly helped me come to my faith in Jesus.

The self-proclaimed atheist is Bob Simon. Bob is a friend of mine and the acclaimed founder of Reston, Virginia. (Robert E. Simon, hence the name Reston.) At the writing of this book, he is the ripe old age of 101! He and I have had many faith talks and he knows that I am praying for him to accept Jesus. Despite our differences, he is always open to talk about faith or any other topic, for that matter. Bob's vision was to design a community of all different races, religions and socioeconomic backgrounds. I benefitted from growing up in a diverse community and it certainly influenced my view of the world. We went to school with kids who lived in mansions with indoor pools and with kids who lived in subsidized housing. I attended a Bar Mitzvah before I went to a Confirmation. Listening and learning different perspectives has always been a very enjoyable part of my life, instilled in me by my years in Reston.

While I knew there was a God and that He was taking care of me, I had no real concept of who Jesus was. I am sure that there were some genuine attempts to explain Him to me, but clearly I was not ready since I did not accept Jesus as Lord and Savior of my life until I was 28. One of the times I do remember someone "witnessing" to me was a turn-off. I was 16, and while I knew there was some truth in what this person was telling me, his racist and anti-Semitic statements discredited him right away. I knew that the God I would serve loved everybody.

The depiction of the Anglo Jesus also bothered me. It made me think that Christianity must be more for white people and that God spoke to different cultures through their different religions. I thought there must be many paths to heaven. Curiously, it was while reading the autobiography of Malcolm X that I received a big revelation. Malcolm X adamantly declared in prison that Jesus was black. When I looked into it more, his position on the matter rang true. We certainly know that Jesus was not Norwegian as the pictures would have you believe. He was Middle Eastern, so we know he had darker skin. While it may sound funny to some of you, this revelation helped me be more open to Jesus' message.

Ravi Zacharias, who is Founder and President of Ravi Zacharias International Ministries (RZIM), says that "a strong stigma always licks (defeats) solid dogma." He is explaining that most of us will only listen to someone with whom we can relate and we will not listen to someone about whom we have certain negative preconceived notions. It could be you do not like, respect or trust someone from a different state or country or race. It could be as simple as you just do not know how to relate to a person who is different from you. All of us have people with whom we can relate and those with whom we cannot.

God had to use many different people to help me understand who Jesus is and certainly had to remove the stumbling blocks that kept me from Him. He wants all people to come to Him. He wants us to know that He created diversity and made each of us to be unique and have our own particular, personal relationship with Him. Through the experiences He allowed in my life, God gave me the idea for this book and the desire to help all people understand how they can be guaranteed their place in heaven.

Through different people, God revealed to me that I was not good enough, no matter how hard I tried, to make it to heaven without a Savior. You and I may be on different ships in life, but we are all in the "same boat." The Bible says that we are all sinners and destined for hell if we do not have Jesus. While that is not a good boat to be in, the good news is that there is a way out, and His name is Jesus. When you have time, read Romans 3:23, Romans 5:8 and Romans 6:23. The most important decision that you and I will ever make in our lives is deciding who Jesus is.

Any time I brought up the concept for this book, I immediately received a very positive response. The question, however, was could we actually bring together a diverse group of believers in Jesus from the Northern Virginia area who would share from their personal perspective how Jesus had profoundly affected each of their lives - from a variety of churches, with denominational, racial, political and cultural differences? Would these people work together to proclaim, with common voice, that Jesus is Lord of All, and the true and only way to heaven?

The answer to this question is shown in the diversity of writers in this book and their message from the Gospel that Jesus came to save us all. Each writer embraced the opportunity, and their only stipulation was that their fellow writers properly portrayed Jesus.

The people who wrote chapters in this book are not perfect. They will be the first to tell you they are far from it. But without exception, they wholeheartedly embraced this project and did not allow ego or the pretext of their different cultural, racial and denominational backgrounds to keep them from being in this book together. We know Rev. Martin Luther King, Jr. once said that the most segregated hour of the week in America is the 11 o'clock hour on Sunday morning, referencing the lack of unity of the Body of Christ when it comes to worshipping together.

The authors of this book have come together for two main reasons. First and foremost, the burning desire for you to understand that Jesus is the Lord of All and that He is your answer to eternity in heaven. Secondly, they want to show that there is, indeed, unity in the Church body when the focus is simply on Christ and Christ alone. While our nation and world are divided on so many levels, we all pray that we can respect people as people and keep the mindset that God loves everyone equally and that we are all equally valuable to God.

We pray that you can relate to one or more people in this book and that you will be inspired to begin or deepen your own personal relationship with Jesus. He truly is Lord of All.

TO GOD BE THE GLORY
Christopher Gnanakan

Was it fate? It must have been predestined for two people from such diverse Indian ethnicities to be drawn to each other. My dad, Guru Manikam Gnanakan, hailed from Tamil Nadu and my mom, Iris Gonzago, was from the state of Kerala and had some Portuguese blood in her! Dad married Mom in Bangalore, Karnataka, where he was employed as a commercial artist by the British Raj at the Indian Tin Industries. Mom taught at the English school that my grandma founded in 1965— the year I was born. My story begins in this "united states of south India" where I was born and bred within a mixed [Tamil-Malayalam-Kanada] culture, surrounded by Hindus and Muslims.

From the *God of Death's Eye* to a *Carrier of Christ*

My grandfather, a Hindu garment trader, was one of the earliest converts to Jesus in his village. He retained his surname, *Gnana*, which in the Tamil language means "knowledge." The word *kan* represents the third "eye" on the forehead of Shiva, the god of death! For eight years my mom was childless, which was commonly deemed a curse. So her mother, who was from a staunch Roman Catholic background, took her to St. Anthony's shrine and vowed that if she had a baby, the child would be dedicated to Christ's service. The next year, Mom had twins! The first baby, unfortunately, died at birth. The other grew up being called a "miracle baby!" Keeping their vow, my parents took me to that shrine and christened me *Christopher* – "bearer of Christ!"

Asia has a high premium on education. We have a goddess named *Saraswati* whose blessing is believed to produce opportunities for learning and, in turn, socio-economic progress. My mom was determined to break the "curse" of poverty that we had found ourselves in since Dad had lost his job. She borrowed money from cruel lenders to get me off the streets and enroll me in Clarence High School, started by Brethren missionaries. Each day during chapel our teachers shared stories of Jesus' compassionate life that I found winsome. What appealed most to me were Jesus' promises to anyone who trusted and followed Him. I was struck by His seemingly arrogant yet bold claim that no one comes to God except through Him. Jesus' uniqueness had gripped my mind.

Pluralistic societies worship many deities and subscribe to two basic concepts. First, every soul (*atman*) is part of the universe and must work out its own destiny toward merging back into god or ultimate reality (*Brahman*). Second, in the Hindu cyclical view of time, the soul is trapped in a cycle of rebirths (reincarnations or *samsara*) with the law of good or bad works (*karma*) within a system of reward or punishment. The notion of salvation (*moksha*) is one of release or liberation from this unending death and rebirth cycle. Yet the Bible teaches that there is only one life and that only faith in Jesus grants *eternal* life here and now! How can one get everything for nothing?!

When attending festivals, you soon realize that Hindu beliefs and practices are varied both at the philosophical and, more so, at the popular level at which society functions. Many gods like *Shiva* or *Vishnu* (the *Sustainer* with incarnations, *avatars* e.g. *Krishna*) are worshipped out of fear or in order to gain favor. Yet technically the millions of manifestations from one supreme, impersonal *Brahman* remain as unknowable forces. There was in my inner being the yearning to know God in such an experiential way that I could make Him known. Daily, my school's motto inscribed across the hall reminded us that "the fear of the Lord is the beginning of wisdom" (Proverbs 9:10). The God of the Bible promised that all who seek Him with all of their heart will find Him. So began my search.

How Dare They Call God "Father"!

A classmate and close friend invited me to Emmanuel Church where I began to discover two unique truths about the Christian faith. While Hindus had thousands of names for their gods and Muslims have some ninety-nine names for Allah, only Christians dare to call God their "Father." I began to perceive the ultimate reality of God as someone real, not an illusion (*maya*) of a weak mind. While reading the Bible, I thought deeply on the implications of the Fatherhood of God. Christians believed in God as Creator, the Source of all life who called everything into existence out of nothing. But beyond this meaningful Creator-creature divide, addressing God as "Father" indicated that people could have a personal relationship with Him. I wondered how this was possible.

While Hindu devotees (*bhaktas*) sought after a deity, among all the faiths I had studied, only the God of the Bible presented Himself as a "seeking God." Further, this God, in sending His Son Jesus as His chosen *Christ* (Anointed One), reached out to humans who were without strength to save themselves! Moreover, I learned that *Jesus*, meaning Savior or *Liberator*, claimed to have come to seek and save sinners or rebels who were God's enemies (Rom. 5:6-10). This, indeed, was good news!

One Sunday afternoon, I dragged my friend to an Indian movie, after which he invited me to an evening "Gospel Service." That night, I understood what Jesus had accomplished on my behalf when He died and rose again. I decided to turn from my sins and follow Jesus as my Lord and *Guru* – the One who had shown me that He was *the Way* (the only *Marga*) to God! Now, it struck me that good people don't go to heaven, only "perfect" people do. When I trusted in God's Son whom He had sent to save me, "perfect" is exactly how God assessed me! It was not about good deeds (*karma*) I earned, nor was it my fate (*kismet*) to remain caged in my sinful life. God's amazing *grace (charis,* undeserved favor) had forgiven me and His Holy Spirit had given me everything for a godly life. I now could call God "my Father!" Because of this vertical relationship, I also found a new horizontal one: my local church became my spiritual family. It was in and through my church as my new faith community that I began to fulfill my true duty (*dharma*, religious role). It was exciting to live out my new identity as a minister of the Gospel of grace.

Good Works: My Christian *Dharma*, Not *Karma*!

As Jesus' *shisya* (disciple), I learned that even He was "attested by God before people with mighty works" (Acts 2:22). Jesus challenged people to believe Him for what He said and claimed to be, or else—for His very work's sake (John 14:11). I made the distinction between doing good works in order to be saved, and good works expected of me as a result of experiencing God's saving grace because of *the* Work of Christ. *Yesu Guru* clearly taught His *bhaktas* that every good tree produces good fruit. This is what unbelievers will know me by, and how they will know that I belong to the Father of all lights. I was saved to serve. True liberation is not trying to do what I can't, but being His workmanship and fulfilling what God created me for "in Christ": the good works that God has ordained for my life.

During my adolescence, soccer, or "real" football, was a vital part of my life. I played on the streets and often got into fights. I had to learn that life is not a playground, but a battlefield. God had given me a keen mind and I did well in college. Yet, being the eldest son in a family with little means, with a father without a steady income, I was forced to find a job. During my first year at Joseph's Science College I was selected as an apprentice for a German motor industries company in India. I worked 9 a.m. to 5 p.m. as an electrician in this factory for four years, earning a stipend to pay house rent. This gave me an industrious, entrepreneurial spirit and exposed me to the struggles and aspirations of the middle class. Long before I studied *The Protestant Ethic and the Spirit of Capitalism* by German author Max Weber, I valued the "work ethic" that dignifies human beings and creates wealth. I worked hard against a culture of unhealthy dependency that impoverishes, and the culture of entitlement that makes us slothful!

My teaching gift was discerned and developed as I served on my church's leadership team. I'm indebted to my pastoral and lay leaders who gave me a platform. Jesus' *calling* is His *enabling*. All religions have precepts with ethics that tell you what to do and what not to do. But Christianity alone, because of Jesus' indwelling, empowering Spirit, gives believers the power (*shakthi*) to do that which is required by God's law. As I yielded to His Spirit, my spiritual gifts had a way of building and extending God's kingdom. I soon realized that God was preparing a bilingual, bi-vocational youth for a special cosmopolitan mission! But first, I needed to respond to Jesus' compelling call. This involved a difficult career choice and priority—electrician or evangelist?

Hardware, Software, Everywhere: *Indians Go Global and Viral!*

In the 1980s, the way forward for organizations was to go international. It was also a time when traditional foreign missionaries were being denied religious visas to work in countries like India. The Word of Life Bible Institute (WOLBI) in New York was eager to recruit internationals. Jack Wyrtzen, its founder, longed to "put God's Word under their belt and God's fire in their heart so they can win their lost at any cost!" God used Gene Tozer, a local missionary and my mentor, and evangelist Wendell Calder, a faculty member at the Institute, to encourage me to this end. In 1985 I left my family, my people, and my job, and through a series of providential events, came to WOLBI in Schroon Lake, NY! Coming to America sparked a yearning to know God through His Word that still burns in me.

Along with knowledge (*gnana*), I've appreciated how Hindus stress three other *margas*, or life-paths: personal devotion to a chosen deity (*bhakti*), discipline or mastery of oneself (*yoga*), and detachment through selfless service (*karma*). Word of Life Bible Institute instilled in me an all-around passion for Christian mission that increased my burden for the only two things that last forever: God's Word and people's souls. I learned the discipline of a daily quiet time, meditating on specific content of what God is saying and applying it to my life. This exercise of "rightly dividing God's word" (2 Tim. 2:15) is totally different from mystical forms of transcendental meditation that empties one's mind or seeks esoteric experiences. In this encounter with God in His Word, I was being changed to be more like Jesus, the living Word.

The scholarship prize I cherish most from WOLBI is the *Sumner Wemp* Award for personal soul winning. Knowledge of God's Word further engaged me in God's work. The more I shared it, the more the power of its words kept changing lives everywhere! Promotion – for Asians a sure sign of "divine blessing" – comes neither from the East nor as a result of being in the West, but from the Lord. This blessing enriches without regret or sorrow. The Lord led me into a wider ministry, yet each year I return to WOLBI, where it all began, to teach Acts and Missions. We need roots and wings! The 2014 WOLBI *Victory Journal* that featured the *Alumnus of the Year* had my testimony as its lead article that was entitled, "Making a Pact for a Global Impact!" God was at work and I happened to be there!

Communicating Christ *across Caste and Class without Corruption*

In 1987, my scholarships made it possible for me to transfer to Tennessee Temple University in Chattanooga, TN. It was a privilege to be taught by great giants of the Baptist denomination. Lee Robertson, Don Jennings, and visiting lecturers like Warren Wiersbe and Wendell Kempton inspired me to learn to become an effective communicator. They infused in me a high view of the Church and of missions. I realized "Readers were leaders;" "The best knowledge remained useless unless communicated well;" and "Everything rises or falls on leadership!" I graduated *summa cum laude* as the class valedictorian, yet was most humbled by the J.R. Faulkner *Christian Servant Award*. It always reminds me that true greatness in leadership is in being a servant. Christians lead by serving others.

Some ideas and practices among American believers troubled me. For instance, the need to belong to a particular denomination, like the Baptists, tended to separate believers from other Christians. Pressure to use a particular Bible translation or external dress codes subtly suggested a higher or holier-than-thou spirituality. Such unwritten codes reminded me of the Indian *caste* system! I was fond of the egalitarian community in Christ that the Gospel produces. Hindus are born into a social hierarchy of castes: *Brahmin* priests, *Kshatriya* ruler-warriors, *Vaisya* business-traders, and *Sudra* menial-cleaners. When pride or prejudice causes division and discrimination among Christians, it brings disgrace to the Gospel. I determined to celebrate the diversity among God's people and maintain our essential unity in Christ, which in itself is our witness for Him.

The blatant sexual immorality and divorce rate among Christians was also deeply disturbing. I was in "the land of the free" but America was issuing licenses to sin. It claimed to be "the home of the brave" yet not many stood up against corruption. Leaders were notorious for misappropriating church funds. I was not unfamiliar with such practices, as in India, some rich Brahmin priests have also used their position and power to keep the common people in ignorance (*agnana*). They have oppressed lower castes and the *dalits*, literally the "crushed," who Gandhi called "children of God." Others have indulged in grave forms of corruption. So, moral and financial issues are transcultural matters of the human heart. Soon after graduation, picking up my educational tools, I returned to India to start my outreach work.

Wholistic Mission amidst the Afflicted and Affluent

Arriving back in India, I was welcomed by my family and the local church from where I had been sent. Like the apostle Paul, "I've always aspired to preach the Gospel where Christ was not known" (Rom. 15:20). The next year, we surveyed Banaswadi, an urbanizing area on the city outskirts. We began planting a church with three families attending a weekly prayer and Bible study. Asian believers bring two distinct gifts to global Christianity: strong family ties and a deep sense of community. We capitalized on these. By using indigenous art forms like choreography, drama, and contemporary music in our worship services, we attracted many young people.

India has unique marriage traditions with regard to matchmaking and dowry. In the West we usually marry the one we love, whereas in India we learn to love the one we marry—a sure call to *agape*, a self-emptying love. At a Christmas cantata, my dad noticed a fine girl he believed would make a good wife for me. Dorothy and I were married on November 10, 1990, a Saturday. That Sunday, I preached at Banaswadi Church and, on the Monday following, we attended a Greek exegesis course at the South Asia Institute for Advanced Christian Studies (SAIACS). From the start, *praxis*, or doing ministry, followed by critically reflecting on and improving our methods, was our mission strategy.

The first ten years of our marriage were hectic. First of all, there was building Banaswadi Church and teaching at SAIACS. Besides church planting, pastoring and lecturing, I had a radio program, *Transforming Truth* and I regularly spoke at city-wide and national conferences. Being passionate for the truth, we named our first daughter Alethea (Greek for *truth*). We soon learned we can be fundamentally truthful, yet hurtful if we fail to be caring. Our second daughter we called Charis (*grace*) to remind us of how God came to us "in Christ"—full of grace *and* truth (John 1:14). Our daughters' names are a constant reminder for us to keep this balance of truth and grace in all our dealings and relationships.

Christianity, if we are not careful, can become a performance or even a religion based on works. We can get caught up in a sort of *samsara* or endless "cycle of works," trying to gain God's favor or win His pleasure. I realized that, long before Jesus started His ministry or performed any miracle, God declared Him as His "beloved, with whom He was well pleased."

Dorothy and I are attentive to the need for mission in the marketplace. The development of software industries in India showed us that we cannot drive a wedge between the so-called *secular* and *sacred*. Mission work was taking place among the persecuted poor and also among those plunged into new forms of prosperity.

At this point, God brought the pastoral-theologian John Stott to SAIACS and into my life. I had earned a doctorate researching the issue of suffering (*dukka*), a common theme in both Hinduism and Buddhism that posits *desire* as its root cause. The problem now in Asia was with the health-and-wealth gospels advocated by "Christian" televangelists. Seconded by Stott, I received a full scholarship to pursue a PhD at Leeds University, UK, exploring the correlation between Christian faith, healing, and prosperity.

Charismata and Compassion: *Equipped and Empowered for Mission*

Our 5-year stay and my studies in the UK proved fruitful. We became cognizant of the fact that God was preparing us for global missions with the best values from both the East and the West. While in Leeds, we served on the pastoral team at the South Parade Baptist Church, opposite the Headingley Cricket Stadium. We were privileged to participate in and contribute to academic, church, and mission initiatives, from lectures at Oxford and Cambridge to *Christians against Poverty* campaigns. Dorothy found her calling or "vocation" besides being a homemaker. She was indeed gifted to train, not in the traditional forms of missionary theology, but in information technology. Using business as a place for mission allows us to be a witness at our workplaces. God was preparing us to serve "the millennials!"

In the UK, we worked to enhance our collaborative—rather than crusading or colonizing—mission methods. Christian education, for me, was about "loving God with all my mind" and the Church, "God's generous kingdom people," and to care for the last, lost, and least in society. We returned to SAIACS in India with two endowments: a mission theology of providence and, without Hindu deterministic views, we could participate as "heirs together," attempting great things for God and expecting great things from God. In Asia, the sacred is not explained as much as experienced and "miracles" or supernatural manifestations are celebrated. Further, the concept of compassion (Greek, *to suffer with*) in Tamil is *manadhurukkam*, literally, the melting of one's heart. This is a highly esteemed virtue. My PhD dissertation, *Charismata & Compassion* (Lambert Academic Press, Germany), argued for the archetypal "wounded healer," showing the missional power of Christian suffering. With this I proposed an "Expo Factor" that focused exponentially on training national trainers, specifically for native, organic mission among *Unreached People Groups*. A lot of theory; however, God was yet to show this missionary how to be a movement mobilizer with these concepts.

I flapped my wings travelling East and West to the Lausanne Movement for world evangelization and trained scores of vanguard leaders at the Haggai Institute International in Singapore and Maui. My mission had gone global and viral! At this juncture, the Spirit poignantly asked, "Are you living your dream or vitalizing Jesus' vision?" I examined how the disciples sought to fulfill Jesus' Great Commission, and I wondered, "How come, with all our knowledge, technology and resources, the job is not yet done?" Then I heard God's voice clearly calling me, this time to do something "lower, wider, and harder!" I wrestled with God trying to discern what this was.

While the West is more conscious of clock-time (*chronos*), non-western worldviews are acutely aware of time in the sense of opportune moments (*kairos*). I was convinced that God had called me to a work that was lower, wider, and harder. But I was uncertain where, how, and most importantly, when. A year after all four of our parents died I was invited to a missions conference in Maine, USA. Here God revealed the details of His call to me. We met with Outreach to Asia Nationals (OTAN), a mission started in Maine by the late Otis Goodwin. Jerry Mick, who I knew well, was serving as Interim Director and he encouraged me to consider serving with them. After hearing me speak and briefly getting to know me, the board also challenged me to join the work of OTAN. Once again, I clearly heard that voice: "lower, wider, and harder!" This organization served in assisting national leaders within resisted access countries in Asia. They needed a new leader and its board was convinced an Asian should now take this on! So "lower" meant to equip grassroots workers; "wider," to leave my academic compound and go to Asia's mission fields; and "harder" was to serve the persecuted churches! Preparation, providence, and purpose converged and flooded my heart as in faith, with Dorothy, I responded to become OTAN's "Director for Training."

Till Jesus Comes, Going and Doing What Others *Don't, Won't, and Can't*

Timing is important. Dorothy and I, typical Indians, lived close to our aging parents to take care of them. In Asian cultures, elders are revered and parents are often considered as "seen gods." In the late 90s when we both lost our parents, we were comforted by two wonderful truths: first, that the Christian God, unlike other unpredictable or capricious gods, was *sovereign*. He is too good to be unkind and too wise to make mistakes in our lives. Also, something is not "lost" if we know where it is! Our parents had each trusted Jesus as their personal Savior, so we knew where they were! The believer's death is referred to as "sleep." Hence, it is not a dead end but a doorway—not to the next cycle of ethical living but to eternal life in Jesus' presence. Second, we trusted in a God who had proved Himself *faithful*, working all things, good and bad, for our good and His glory! However, this promise holds good only for those who love Jesus and demonstrate this by obeying His call.

Coming back to America was a daunting experience. This time, with our teenage daughters, we left everything to relocate from Bangalore to Bangor with two suitcases each! The Bangor Baptist Church welcomed us into their families and showed us such hospitality! I'm convinced this is the most effective missionary strategy and sadly the "missing jewel" in Western ministry. Dorothy taught at Bangor Christian School and as an IT trainer at the University of Maine. We are persuaded that life is not about prosperity, but spiritual posterity. We want to leave a legacy of faith. Our girls were adjusting to schools and making new friends. Not neglecting our home as my primary parish, I travelled to train nationals in restricted access nations: China, Vietnam, Laos, Cambodia, Nepal, Bhutan, etc. In the process of going "From Good to Great," the board knew more changes were needed. I was asked to be OTAN's Executive Director. We moved to our head office in Winchester, Virginia. Now the axiom "everything rises or falls on leadership" weighed even heavier on me!

Our faith is not fate or based on human explanations. It is a living and personal relationship with the God of the Bible who fulfills His promises and provides for His children. Our eldest daughter joined the pre-med college at Liberty University in Lynchburg, VA. While visiting her, the faculty requested me to lecture on "evangelizing people of other faiths, and cross-cultural communication in missions." Liberty's leadership inquired about my work with OTAN. With our changing times and needs, they were looking for lecturers with academic, practical, and missional experience. In May 2014, I was appointed as the Professor for Theology and Global Missions, requiring me to commute every Tuesday and Thursday to teach there. I consider myself a living bridge of grace and truth, for now, between the spiritually resourced and the unreached people groups.

I'm fully satisfied being in the center of God's will—in the place where God wants me, doing what He has called and equipped me to do. I have relocated about ten times and often remember that, as missionaries, we are "pilgrims," considered "strangers" on earth. The truth is that with Jesus Christ, my Lord and Savior, I have all that I need and God's grace has given me more than I deserve! There's an

Asian proverb I really like that says, "If you want to go fast, travel alone; if you want to go far, journey together!" I'm thankful to my family, church, and friends who have encouraged, helped, and accompanied me on this adventure of faith. Did my grandmother or parents know that when they named me *Christopher, bearer of Christ*, that someday this child would be leading a mission organization to unreached people within restricted countries in Asia, or training theologians and missionaries at the world's largest Christian university? All this is absolutely the Lord's doing and indeed is marvelous in our eyes! To God be the glory!

Dr. Chris Gnanakan is originally from Bangalore, South India, and now lives with his family in Chantilly, VA. Married for 25 years to Dorothy, an educational consultant, they have two daughters, Alethea and Charis. Chris has a passion to teach Global Studies and to motivate and mobilize leaders for missions in Asia. He also loves humor, cross-cultural travel, playing football (soccer), and memorizing poems.

Chris is currently Professor of Theology & Global Studies at Liberty University School of Divinity. Chris holds a D.D. in Mission Theology and Church Leadership from Trinity Baptist College, a PhD in Theology and Religious Studies from Leeds, and a D.Min in Pastoral Theology and Missiology from SAIACS in India.

Chris also serves as the Executive Director of Outreach to Asia Nationals (OTAN), a mission organization focused on reaching the least-reached in restricted-access countries in Asia. As director, Chris is able to fulfill his passion and calling to train leaders in Asia for missions, enabling nationals to reach nationals with the Gospel.

ENTERING GOD'S KINGDOM
Mike Minter

Everyone who enters this world eventually finds him or herself standing before a smorgasbord of ideas, truth claims, religions, philosophies, and a host of other voices saying, "Pick me, pick me." Each voice has an appeal. Your choice will dictate the storyline of your life. One thing is for certain… you have a story.

Here is mine.

I came into this world seventy years ago. By God's grace, I had the unique privilege of being raised in a wonderful home with loving parents who gave me a firm foundation on which to build a healthy life of integrity and strong moral convictions. It wasn't perfect but it was about as good as it gets. My dad graduated from the United States Naval Academy in 1937 and eventually became a three-star admiral and Superintendent of the Academy in the early sixties.

I had a great deal of exposure to traveling and meeting many people from all walks of life which has served me well in social settings I would otherwise not have developed. My mom was devoutly religious and my dad mildly so. He was more intellectual and developed a skeptical view of religious matters early in his life.

His skepticism became firmly rooted at the early age of eight. While in church one Sunday, the pastor gave an old fashioned altar call by telling those who wanted Jesus that they would find him up front. To an eight-year-old mind, that literally meant that Jesus would be there waiting for him when he came forward. As the pastor was counseling others who had made their way up front, my dad kept looking for Jesus but saw no signs of Him anywhere. He even looked behind the pulpit, but no Jesus.

Thus began his first encounter with religion and the birth of his own skepticism. He saw all this as a hoax, even though he came from a very strong Christian home. I have never forgotten my dad telling me that story and how much it impacted his life. It was a defining moment and one that stuck with him over the years.

All of us are impacted by our parents, and my upbringing was no different. I was being raised by an intellectual skeptic and a devoutly religious mother – though they had both agreed early on in their marriage that this would never become a contentious issue nor would it be table conversation over dinner. My mom made sure that all three kids would be in church every week.

As I began to start thinking on my own, I started asking questions similar to my dad's. The answers I got were threadbare, empty, and manufactured. The tough questions were usually met with, "That's a great mystery, my son." I needed more than that to sustain me when it came to the real issues of life. In January of 1970, I was contacted by a young man who had just returned from Vietnam. We had known each other in college but more as acquaintances and not as good friends.

Bruce invited me over to his apartment for dinner one evening and when I arrived I was quite surprised to find a very organized and neat environment. Not what I had expected from a young bachelor.

On top of the coffee table was a Bible, which I thought a bit strange. A men's magazine, yes, but a Bible? I still remember what he served. It was roast beef, and before we plowed into the food he said grace. The prayer was not memorized but seemed to come from a man who knew God personally.

We became fast friends and he suggested we take off the month of June and head for Europe. The cheapest and most flexible way to travel was by train, so we purchased tickets that gave us unlimited travel. The Lord was tilling the soil and laying the groundwork for me to hear the gospel. I thought we were on a vacation but the truth, from heaven's perspective, was that I was on a spiritual journey. It was a heavenly ambush. I became quickly aware that my friend Bruce knew God in a way that seemed almost foreign to me. We ran into many obstacles as we traveled and Bruce would simply pray out loud, invoking the power of Christ to handle the situation. I realize the word "miracle" is sometimes overused in Christian circles, but I have to tell you that I had never seen such immediate answers to prayer in all my life. I almost said, "Take me to your leader," but managed to suppress the notion.

Clearly, the Lord was getting my attention. I started asking questions and Bruce started giving me answers from the Scriptures. Nothing was based on opinion but was substantiated by God's Word. While in Spain, he handed me a copy of the New Testament called *Good News for Modern Man*, published by The Fellowship of Christian Athletes. He told me to start reading the gospel of John. Traveling from one country to the next afforded me much time to read and reflect. By the time we reached Copenhagen, Denmark I had completed my assignment.

Though I don't recall all the questions I asked him, Bruce well remembers me wanting to call upon the Lord for my salvation. So in a small Bed and Breakfast, I confessed my need for Christ *alone* to save me and give me everlasting life. My entire world was turned upside down. This was not some short-term emotional experience. The whole direction of my life had taken a U-turn.

Upon arriving back in the States, I simply couldn't contain my excitement. However, it wasn't long before mixed emotions began to set in. I had no doubt about my conversion but I did feel somewhat betrayed. Why had no one ever told me this before? Surely I had come across true believers in my twenty-six years of life. Did they feel this was a secret to be kept to themselves? Did they simply not see it as important? Was it not politically correct to discuss such matters? I was deeply troubled by the nonchalance of believers over an eternal issue.

This became a burning passion of mine. If this is such great news how could I not tell the world? So my spiritual journey began. I moved from Maryland to Florida and went into the life insurance business in South Miami. As I entered people's homes to talk to them about their need for my product, I felt compelled to engage them in spiritual conversation about Life Assurance. My heart was deeply divided between the worlds of business and ministry. In January of 1971, another defining moment interrupted the trajectory of my life.

While leaving the office one evening, I met a young lady who had been recently hired to answer the phones. We struck up a conversation and I soon found out that she was attending a local Bible college. She invited me to a Wednesday night concert, and I gladly accepted. While at the college I noticed a flyer introducing some nighttime Bible courses. Since I knew practically nothing about the scriptures, I signed up. Those night classes set my heart on fire to know more. Was this book actually inspired? What about other spiritual books from other religions? My appetite for answers was that of a lion searching for wildebeests on the Serengeti. But who would hold my hand and lead me in this new adventure?

Through a series of events I was introduced to Rudy, who was one of the young students preparing for ministry. His passion for the things of God and his insatiable appetite to teach me all he knew became the launching pad for an adult Bible study. By this time I had lost all interest in selling life insurance. My new assignment was to invite as many of my unbelieving friends to the study and it was Rudy's job to teach them. After a while, he informed me that he was graduating and I would have to take over the study. This was equivalent to asking someone who had been on a plane to take the controls of a 747. Panic ensued as I was such a novice regarding spiritual matters and knew very little about the Bible. I was at the deep end of the pool with no lifeguard in sight. But like it or not, there was no one else to take the study.

The very first night that I taught, I felt like Eric Liddell in *Chariots of Fire* who said, "When I run, I feel His pleasure." I felt God's pleasure when I taught. As I drove home that night, I literally heard God tell me, "This is what I want you to do the rest of your life." My mission had been confirmed sitting in my little black Volkswagen Beetle.

Within a few days, I set up a meeting with my boss and told him that I was going to start attending Florida Bible College and prepare for the ministry. He gave me his blessing and I soon enrolled. I spent the next two years, from 1972 to 1974, immersed in the Word. While there I met Kay, the woman who would become my wife, and we were married in 1973. In 1974, I graduated at the age of thirty and we set out on an adventure that I never would have dreamed of.

We were invited to plant a church in Reston, Virginia. We had no source of income and about $700 to our name. But off we went in obedience to the call upon our lives to do something we knew nothing about: plant a church. A dear couple allowed us to use their home as a place to have a Bible study in which to launch what is now Reston Bible Church. There was one big hurdle: I didn't know anyone in Reston. I needed to get a job soon in order to support myself and to meet people that I could invite to the study.

I was able to get a job at the local country club as a glorified locker room attendant. Little did I know that this humbling experience would be the base camp in which to set up shop. I had lunch daily with different people who worked at the club and I invited them to our first study, which was to take place in June, just a month after arriving in Reston. This seemed like a very aggressive plan but I didn't want to waste time. The first night, three people from the club showed up, along with another couple that were friends of the people who allowed us to use their home.

I spoke on the authority of the Bible. It was a basic message on how you could know the Bible was, in fact, the very word of God. I also gave a simple gospel message that night, telling people of the saving grace of Jesus Christ. My first convert arrived early the next morning in the men's locker room. He was also the manager of the club and felt safe in talking to me about the message I had given the previous night. There were no other people at that early morning hour that might interrupt our conversation. Sitting there amongst clubs and cleats, he called upon the Lord to save him.

Needless to say, as the study grew in attendance, much discussion and debate took place, but one by one, the gospel penetrated the hearts of those who attended. As the weeks unfolded, the living room began to swell with people and, in March of 1975, we had our first Sunday service with about twenty-five in attendance. Week after week, new people showed up. Because most of the attendees were new believers, they had a passion to share the good news of Jesus with their friends and so invited them to come to our services.

Over the years, RBC began to develop a heart for missions well beyond the borders of the USA. Why keep this good news to ourselves? I was soon challenged to visit a foreign field and my first mission trip was to the jungles of Bolivia. What a way to get baptized into the world of global evangelization! Ever since that first trip, I have had a heart for people all over the globe, but there is a special place in my heart for the jungle and its people. Though I have taken about twenty-five trips to a wide variety of places, the Lord, for whatever reason, has given me a heart for the many people groups along the Amazon River.

I am now involved in a mission called JMI which stands for Justice and Mercy International. Every year, and sometimes twice a year, I head off to the Amazon where I train pastors who serve in villages up and down this mighty river. This is where I really get energized to see the power of the gospel set people free from spirit worship, voodoo and a host of other false teachings that have held people captive most of their lives.

Each time I return, I get a report from the pastors who tell me how much the teaching has helped them carry God's truth back to their people. However, I always remind them that they are my heroes. Their lives are difficult but their trust in the Lord far overshadows mine. *I know the Bible better than they do but they know the Jesus of the Bible better than I do.* Here again, we find people in hidden parts of the world who have had their lives dramatically changed by the power of Christ.

I started this chapter by saying there are many offers on the spiritual landscape, but there is only one Jesus. Since I am living in what I call the intellectual capital of the world (the Washington, DC area), and travel to places where people have never been to school, I have a pretty good sense of the power of God's good news about His Son. Many philosophies, religions, sects and cults require a certain amount of training just to understand the system. However, the gospel of Christ is simple to understand. Perhaps this is why Jesus said, *"Truly I tell you, anyone who will not receive the kingdom of God like a little child will never enter it"* (Mark 10:15 NIV).

Run any belief system through this grid and see if it is that simple. Only the pure gospel of Jesus is uncomplicated. This is why the word gospel means "good news." It is not good news to be told that you must live a good life in order to be accepted by God because we would fail to meet the measure of perfection. It is because we are *not* perfect that we need a Savior, and that he has come to save us from our sins and weaknesses is the center of the gospel message.

This has been the center of my preaching over the years. It has shaped the entire ministry of RBC. I want people everywhere to know and understand the simplicity of the gospel. I have been passionate about making it very clear. The skeptic and unbeliever need to hear the gospel clearly presented. The apostle Paul put it like this: "If the trumpet gives an uncertain sound who will prepare himself for the battle? (1 Cor. 14:8 NIV)."

I close every service with a clear gospel message of salvation and I can't tell you how many people over the years have told me they came to know Christ by only visiting RBC once and then heading off to college or moving to another state. This has nothing to do any inherent power in me. The power is in the gospel itself. Paul again speaks when he says, "For the gospel is the power of God unto salvation to everyone who believes" (Rom.1:16 NIV). This has been one of the great joys of my life.

I recently had a man come up to me after one of our services and say, "I just wanted to say thanks." I said, "For what?" He then told me how, thirty-three years ago when he was in high school, he came to one of our services because he knew a pretty girl who attended, and he wanted to meet her. She was not there that day but he heard the gospel and believed it. He then proceeded to tell me how it ruined his life. I looked a bit perplexed. "My plans," he said, "were to go off to college and be the biggest partier on campus, but the good news of Jesus spared me from that and I have been following Him ever since." What a joy to see a life changed. No philosophy or religion has that kind of instantaneous power. The actual good news of Jesus transformed his life and set a new direction without any training. I am not opposed to training, but the power is in the person of Christ. He and He alone can change the direction of a life in a split second.

One of my favorite stories about changed lives happened many years ago when a young man came into my office asking me what I believed about Jesus. He then wanted to know if he and some of his friends could start attending RBC. I assured him they were all welcome. One of his friends had been separated from his wife for two years. They were headed for divorce. He attended but she wanted nothing to do with going to the same church. After some coaxing, she came in to see me. She agreed to let her husband back into the house. This was 1980. Their marriage was healed and he went on to serve as an elder at RBC and now pastors a local church.

Another couple had one of the worst marriages I have ever encountered. To make matters worse, they struggled with a rebellious son. After understanding the gospel, the entire family was turned around. The son ended up on the mission field and the father is on staff at a local Bible church. We aren't quite finished. Yet another one of the couples got very involved in the church - he became an elder and now they have planted a church in the area. The young man who first came in to see me became our youth pastor and is now a counselor in South Carolina. What a ride it has been to see wrecked lives put back together. The gospel is not just for one kind of person. It transcends all time and all cultures.

So to wrap things up, my life was turned around the moment the gospel took hold of my heart. All things became new the moment I realized that entering God's Kingdom had nothing to do with my human goodness but everything to do with Christ's righteousness, which is given as a gift to anyone who will call upon Him to save their soul. It gave me a passion to see others come to this truth. The whole purpose behind this book, of which my chapter is one part, is to let you see how this good news impacts lives from Capetown to Calcutta, from Chicago to Shanghai, from Naples to Nepal, from our hearts to yours. Do you know Him?

Mike Minter was born into a Navy family in Providence, Rhode Island, in 1944. He is the son of an Admiral and himself attended the Naval Academy, later obtaining a degree in Political Science from Old Dominion University. He graduated from Florida Bible College in 1974. It was at FBC that he met and married his wife, Kay, and was called to the ministry to start an evangelical work in Reston where he still serves as the senior pastor of Reston Bible Church.

His first book, entitled A Western Jesus, *takes a fresh look at what it means to follow Christ. Now in his fourth decade of ministry, Pastor Minter is a coveted speaker. He is known for his great insight into God's Word, keen ability to communicate it in a way that is relevant to the 21st century believer, and his appeal to both adults and youth in all stages of their walk with Christ. Mike and Kay live in Virginia, and have four grown children and a growing number of grandchildren.*

THE DIFFERENCE THE GOSPEL MAKES
Alice Kim

The gospel is said to be the greatest love story between God and His creation. God willingly gave up His comfort, power, and position and came in the form of a man. His name is Jesus.

During His thirty-plus years on earth, He taught with wisdom, cared for people through miraculous healings, and led by humble example. His ultimate act of love was displayed on the cross as He hung there for the world to see. He did all this to rescue us from the darkness that is in each of us. His perfect life and death bridged the gap between our inability to guarantee goodness no matter how great our efforts, and God's perfect goodness. He made a way to restore the broken relationship that existed ever since its severing in the Garden of Eden.

If we say yes to God's love, He calls us His sons and daughters. If we acknowledge our inability to earn his love on our own merits, He promises to be a Father to us who will never leave or forsake us. He will always act in kindness toward us.

I believe in this gospel. Yet there are times when the question – what difference does the gospel make? – is not far from my thoughts.

I am a mom of two elementary school-aged girls who are quickly nearing adolescence, a wife of a local church pastor, a student of His Word, and a Christian psychotherapist in private practice. In each of these spheres of life, I encounter experiences and stories that cause me to wrestle with this very question.

I struggle to know how the gospel makes a difference when I am confronted by the folly of my heart, when I am consumed by efforts to build a fortifying wall of safety and protection, and when taking another step seems insurmountable.

In my work, I am invited into places where suffering and tragedy are inescapable. For example, where profound loneliness is like an uninvited guest who overstays his welcome; where tenderness and intimacy are scarce commodities in a barren relationship; where a marriage is held together by a thin thread of perfunctory roles and duties; where hatred, evil, and violence ravage communities; where tragic death permanently severs any sense of closeness; where shame and contempt hijack a heart; and where voices of unworthiness, unloveability, failure and displeasure haunt the soul. In circumstances like these, what difference does the gospel make?

The image surrounding Jesus' birth is one that was formed from many years of Sunday School attendance. Commercialized seasonal cards reinforced it. It is one of bliss and tranquility. But the first four books of the New Testament tell a far more disturbing account.

It was a time of displacement. Families left their homes to comply with the census ruling. Jesus was born in an ad hoc shelter. His birth aroused King Herod's jealousy that led to the massive killing of infant boys two years old and under. It was far from the Hallmark rendering of Christmas.

From the beginning, Jesus is acquainted with chaos, poverty, injustice, and death. Even as He nears the cross, there is no relief to the heartache His life knew all too well. The last days of His life are plagued with significant brutality, abandonment, humiliation, and deep sorrow.

Jesus cries out in anguish and surrender, "Father, if you are willing, remove this cup from me. Nevertheless, not my will, but yours, be done." (Luke 22:42 ESV) Jesus was stripped naked. If He had any covering, it was a mere loincloth to cover His exposed genitals. He was made a spectacle. With what breath He had remaining, He implores for a response, "My God, my God, why have You forsaken me?" (Matthew 27: 46 ESV) There is only the sound of dreadful silence.

If, in one's most vulnerable state, it is absence that greets you, then what hope is there?

I grew up in the home of an immigrant family with my dad, mom, and older brother. When I was six years old, my parents decided to move halfway across the world to a foreign land where people looked, smelled, sounded, and acted different. We packed up all our belongings into eight four-foot duffle bags. The uncertainty that awaited us was daunting. Thankfully, connections between our home church in Korea and one in Canada helped ease the transition. Our new ethnic church quickly took center stage. It was where we gained information for our livelihood. It played an integral part in our weekly rhythm and social calendar.

Seven years later, the message of Jesus was presented at a Christian youth retreat. Although I had heard it countless times prior, this time it felt much more personal.

Jesus died to save *me*, a sinner. He loves *me*, Alice. He invites *me* to be His child.

What were once fantastic stories that made jaws drop open or minds swirl in endless questions of incredulity now served to showcase a powerful God who was mindful of *me*. Stories like the ark rescuing man- and animal-kind from extinction during forty days and forty nights of continuous rain; a nation freed from slavery crossing a body of water on dry ground without one casualty; one child's lunch feeding thousands of famished stomachs; healing a leper's lifetime of disease and discrimination; and the list goes on. My heart responded with overwhelming gratitude and uncontainable joy.

The Gospel of Luke tells the story of two followers of Jesus. They were leaving the tomb where Jesus' body was laid to rest, except there was no body to mark his death. There was much confusion and despair as they made their way to the town of Emmaus. It was here, on this road, that Jesus showed up.

He asked about their long faces and heavy hearts. They were stunned by Jesus' question. The absurd nature of His inquiry and His ignorance to the local headlines caused them to assume that He was a visitor to the area.

Jesus clearly knew all things but He intentionally proceeded with, "What things?" How did you get here? What road and terrain have you traveled? What has led to your gloom, despair, and hopelessness?

The road to Emmaus was about a seven-mile journey. With His simple yet profound question, He invites them to tell their story for the next seven miles. He walks with them starting from where they are. He sets the tone and pace for their conversation. Their physical destination symbolizes the process of arriving. But it is when their hearts are renewed with hope that transformation occurs.

This, too, is my story.

On any given Sunday at our church, the children worshipped separately in English while the parents worshipped in their native tongue. But this Sunday, the youth joined the adult Korean service.

I was thirteen years old. I walked into the sanctuary that morning and noticed how the room was brightly lit and warmed by the sunrays that seeped through the stained glass window. I took my seat near the front nook with the rest of the youth group. I stood on cue, joined in corporate singing of hymns (in Korean) and I respectfully bowed my head during prayers. Once the message was underway, I began to exchange notes with friends as discreetly as I could. Then the words of the pastor caught my attention.

He posed a precarious scenario and selected my dad for the illustration.

If the entire family (my mom, brother, and I) was drowning in the middle of an ocean and my dad could save only one person, who would he choose?

I quickly scanned the sanctuary for my family. I could spot my dad in the front center pews. Deep grooves around his eyebrows and forehead framed his face. He had his eyes closed in a pensive state. I am not sure where my mom was. Maybe she was seated next to him. I do not recall. I could not locate my brother, either.

The air was somber. No one moved, perhaps in fear of being called into the spotlight along with my dad. Or they were playing the dilemma in their mind and thinking of their own response. Perhaps others were empathizing with the enormity of the pressure my dad was under.

With every second of silence that passed, my insecurity intensified. My heart was pounding so loud that I feared I would miss my dad's response. I took deep breaths to pacify my angst. I stilled my body. My legs that were prone to shaking with nerves were held tightly in place. I put on a smile to divert attention away from how desperately I longed to be chosen.

Given the scenario, rescuing my life would be at the cost of my mom and brother. That would be a tragedy. But my heart fought to know I was worth saving. I argued that I was his only daughter and the youngest in the family. Pick me.

My attempts to conceal my desires and fears were futile. Before my dad could respond, I blurted out, "Me!" Giggles erupted around me. My friends attributed my behavior to adolescence. I was unfazed. My life was in jeopardy.

Daringly, I turned to focus on my dad. I reached past the pews that separated us with my eyes. I scanned his body for any signs that would indicate his acknowledgment of my heart. However, his face remained stoic and his body composed. Then, with resolve in his voice, he announced his decision: "My son."

No explanation followed. No insight into his intent or deliberation or even how every fiber of his being wanted to protest giving an answer. Silence.

There was no longer any ounce of strength or curiosity to glance in his direction. Besides, if our eyes met, what would he communicate – an apology, sorrow, or regret? What would I express – shock, embarrassment, consolation, or assurance that I was okay?

In a desperate attempt to be seen, I had revealed my heart. I was afraid that not risking would be a far greater cost. I was wrong.

In the Asian culture, it is understood that you are loved if you have shelter, home-cooked meals, and material goods to satisfy both needs and wants. As long as there is no overt mistreatment, children are to be grateful for their parents' sacrifice. It is dishonoring to doubt their love especially if they have forgone personal comfort and social status and risked being marginalized and the subject of racism for the sake of a better future for their children. Yet, the cultural explanations did little to soothe the pain.

Color and warmth flooded my face. I forced a smile. I worked harder to maintain it. I was not going to let anyone, especially my dad and my family, see the inner mayhem. It was important that people knew that I was unscathed by the decision. I responded with comments about my resiliency and strength. I joked about my ability to save myself and scoffed at the idea of needing to be rescued. I successfully manipulated the outcome to neutralize the sting of rejection. In the process, I saved face, both my dad's and mine, dissolving any embarrassment this hypothetical dilemma had created. Honor and dignity were restored.

The choice to pick my brother over me or even over my mom validated what I had suspected for some time but fought so hard to accept. In Confucianism, it is believed that men are more highly valued and favored than women. This thought was passed down from one generation to the next and had permeated my family's dynamics.

The initial shock turned into hurt, hurt aroused shame, and shame evolved into a firmer resolution to be cautious about vulnerability and trust. I was wary of others' influences for ill but also for good. I vowed to not be so foolish as to desire being chosen, known, and treasured. Self-sufficiency became my motto. It fueled a personal commitment to avoid rejection and abandonment. This approach to life fit in well with the Western value that highly regards independence.

I often wondered what had prompted the pastor to paint such a bleak dilemma and then to single out a congregant. I doubt he had any inkling that his query would leave such an indelible mark. In the years since that Sunday, I have not thought of my childhood church as anything but a gospel-centered community. I credit my curiosity about spirituality to this community's influence, especially during the earlier formative years of my faith. Yet the results of that fateful Sunday permeate how I approach life and relationships.

I spent my childhood, my 20s, and even a part of my 30s, waiting for my parents to meet my needs for acceptance and importance. There remained a little girl in me that could not articulate the deep desires of the heart. Beyond the protective exterior wall I had erected lay a hunger to have certain truths spoken over my life. "You matter. Your life is worth being chosen."

Several years ago, I came to realize that I had to release my parents from the unspoken expectations that they themselves were unaware of. It was time. They will always be my parents. No one can take their place. Nevertheless, I had to give voice to my longings to be valued, chosen, and cared for and to grieve what had been absent, so that my heart would begin the journey to freedom. I also had to let go of the personal responsibility I had taken to save face. It was not mine to bear. It was okay to let this go.

The Korean word for "Dad" or "Daddy" is "Abba." This is how I've always known him. But as I bless my dad for both his failures and his successes as a parent, I can find renewed hope in my "Abba Father," my Heavenly Father.

I do long for a day when my parents and I can weep together over our brokenness and speak healing words over the scarred places of our hearts. Oh, how sweet that day will be! But whether that day is tomorrow or in heaven, Jesus invites me to open my heart's door to hope boldly and love courageously.

During a visit to Spain, I noticed a wooden chair carved in the shape of a hand at the residence where we were staying. The four fingers formed the backrest, the thumb became the armrest, the palm of the hand was the seat, and the wrist formed the supporting leg. The realistic resemblance to a hand made me more inclined to admire the artwork from afar than to take respite in it.

One morning, as I noticed the empty chair, I was struck by how difficult it is for me to rest in someone's care. The wooden hand symbolized God's call to press into Him – His goodness, strength, gentleness, faithfulness and trustworthiness. Isaiah describes how God's hand bears the marking of those He loves, "I have engraved you on the palms of my hands" (49:16).

I struggle with fear of rejection, unavailability, and silence. The potential for humiliation gnaws at me. I am terrified at the thought of being caught being foolish again. I guard my heart. It is then that I am gently reminded of a God who draws me to Himself and promises security and safety.

He quiets my panic-stricken heart. "Can a woman forget her nursing child, that she should have no compassion on the son of her womb? Even these may forget, yet I will not forget you." (Isaiah 49:15 ESV) He soothes my tense body. "'For I know the plans I have for you,' declares the LORD, "plans to prosper you and not to harm you, plans to give you hope and a future." (Jeremiah 29:11 ESV). I am able to catch my breath and sink confidently into the reality that my identity – who I am and whose I am – is anchored in Him.

As a result of human depravity and our inability to save ourselves, Jesus absorbed the wrath of God once and for all. It cost Him everything. Jesus entered the ultimate battle against evil so that

He could rescue us from our own version of war and suffering. We do not have to live in a perpetual, vicious cycle. We do not have to labor incessantly to cover up failures, fears, and insecurities with achievements, materialism, personality, fine appearance, and an image of imperviousness. In exchange, Jesus offers freedom and grace. He redeems the once horrible things by weaving them back into our lives, but this time, with chords of hope. The gospel invites us to trust Him by opening our heart to pleasure and delight and to loving others and being loved by others.

The prerequisite is confessing, "I can't." It is only when we arrive at this point that we can hear, "He can." It is a point of surrender and vulnerability. It can be terrifying. But it is the start of a journey that promises life in abundance (John 10:10).

Michael Card, in *A Sacred Sorrow*, writes, "True worship begins in the wilderness. Praise is almost always the answer to a plea that arises in the desert.... There is no worship without wilderness. There can be no worshipful joy of salvation until we have realized the lamentable wilderness of what we were saved from, until we begin to understand just what it cost Jesus to come and find us and be that perfect provision in the wilderness."

So, what difference does the gospel make?

Because of the gospel, we have hope to entrust ourselves to what seems like silence because Jesus entrusted himself by taking his last breath into the silence of God.

Because of the gospel, we have hope to believe what Paul writes in his letter to the Roman believers, "For I am sure that neither death nor life, nor angels, nor rulers, nor things present, nor things to come, nor powers, nor height, nor depth, nor anything else in all creation, will be able to separate us from the love of God in Christ Jesus our Lord." (Romans 8:38-39 ESV)

Because of the gospel, we have courage to look death in the face and say with confidence, "O death, where is your victory? O death, where is your sting?" (1 Corinthians 15:55 ESV)

Death is not the end. It does not have the final word. Resurrection follows death. And hope is found in Jesus' ascension to resume His place at the right hand of God the Father where He is interceding for you and me (Romans 8:34). He departs, but not without leaving us with a gift. The Holy Spirit is with us. We are never left stranded or deserted. There is also the future promise of Jesus' return for a final reunion and to take us home to our heavenly destination where all fears are relieved and all desires fulfilled. This is good news!

This is my story.

Alice Kim is a Licensed Clinical Social Worker in Virginia and offers gospel-centered therapy at Emmaus Counseling and Consulting Services (www.emmausccs. com). She opened her practice in 2008. Prior to this, she worked for Fairfax-Falls Church Community Service Board, Community Mental Health. She finds deep fulfillment entering into people's stories and discovering hope and freedom. She currently serves in leadership at Western-Fairfax Community Bible Study as an Associate Teaching Director and is involved in her church, Great Commission Community Church located in Arlington and Tysons Corner. She is married to Sam who serves as an Associate Pastor at their church. He never ceases to make her laugh and continues to remind her daily of God's goodness. They have been married for over 14 years and raise two daughters.

MY JOURNEY TO THE AMERICAN DREAM
Carlos Penaloza

My name is Carlos Penaloza. I have been a pastor for over 40 years, and this is my story.

I am originally from Bolivia, a beautiful country in the heart of South America. While Bolivia has been blessed with abundant natural resources and breathtaking natural beauty, political instability is also an everyday issue that we have come to accept as part of life.

My journey to become an American was not intentional, nor was it motivated by the typical quest for the American dream. Rather, I came to this wonderful country seeking medical help for my family. Bolivia, like most developing countries, is far behind America in the field of healthcare and medical treatments.

My daughter, Sarita, had been suffering from a terrible skin inflammation that no one in my country was even able to diagnose, let alone treat effectively. We knew that it was imperative to get her to America where the healthcare professionals would surely be able to determine the cause of the inflammation and provide treatment.

When I arrived with my wife and children at Ronald Reagan Airport back in November of 1996, we thought we were coming for about two months, as this was how long they had told us Sarita's treatments would take.

By this time we had learned that all our children had a rare genetic illness called *Ataxia Telangiectasia*, which was inherited from both my wife and me as we were both, unfortunately, carriers of the gene which caused the disease. This diagnosis was given by a pediatrician in 1994 at Johns Hopkins Hospital in Bethesda, Maryland. It was confirmed by a team of scientists in New York doing research into rare diseases such as this. We were blessed to have met these doctors who educated us in how to manage the illness. By this time, we knew that it was incurable and affected a number of systems in the body, mainly the immune system, and that my children were in danger of dying from any sickness, even a cold, because their immune systems were not strong enough, and in one case almost nonexistent.

This experience gave us the opportunity to participate in American life and to actually get to know American people in "the land of the free and the home of the brave."

When we met some of the doctors who were going to take care of my precious Sarita, the kindness and sympathy they showed was a completely new experience for us, as in our country we had so often encountered an apathetic attitude from doctors. Our confidence in these new doctors was also bolstered by the wealth of information they gave us with every treatment she had to endure, and we found that we had the right to refuse any treatment if we thought that it was not the best for our daughter.

Another thing that we found here was the openness from other Christian ministers and the opportunity they gave us to share our story with their congregations. And surprisingly, after every meeting where we shared our testimony, the pastors would very generously give us an offering. That was absolutely unexpected for me, because back in my country we almost never received an offering when invited to speak or preach. I would give the envelope to my wife, without even opening it, and a number of envelopes gathered in a shoebox that my wife kept until we would decide what to do with it.

As the days went by, we learned step-by-step how to navigate through various hospital procedures, and by the time the treatment was over, we had spent every dollar we brought with us, yet the doctors in the hospital told us that they needed to do further studies on my daughter in order to find the cause of the problem in Sarita's skin. I told them we did not have more money to cover further expenses. Amazingly, their response was that they could not let my daughter go without the treatment she needed, so they went ahead and continued to help us, with all the doctors agreeing not to charge for their services. I realized then that generosity was another characteristic of the people of the land of the free and home of the brave. The only bills we received from then on were the ones from the hospital itself.

A few days later, we were informed that the cause of the skin problem – and it went deeper than the skin – was a malignant lymphoma in the bone marrow of my daughter. This report was very hard to handle, as this particular type of lymphoma is usually found only in men over 60 years old, and is only curable with six doses of chemotherapy. The specialists were very surprised with the finding, because this was the first time they found this lymphoma in a six-year-old girl, and they had no protocol to follow for her. So they decided that they would arrange to apply the same treatment given to the adult men, only customized for a girl her age and weight. They also arranged for a couple of extra treatments to her blood. Almost immediately, the results were visible; after the first dose of chemotherapy she started showing changes in her skin. She was much more alert, and great hope started building in our hearts; then the second dose came, and she was doing even better. By now we felt confident to start making plans to go back to my country where a mega church of 12,000 people was waiting for us, where we were part of the pastoral team and where we were much needed.

One day in particular, Sarita was not cooperative with her treatment, as it had become very difficult for her. It was the winter of 1996. She was in her second dose of chemotherapy. She had to wear a mask and her contact with people was minimal because the chemo had made her immune system even weaker.

I had to bribe her to accept the necessary procedure. I said, "If you let them take your blood (which included a needle in her arm), I will send you and your mom to the mall and you can buy anything that you want." She replied, "Okay," with a smile.

When she came back from the mall, she had bought a beautiful blue dress, a white hat and white gloves.

That night we had a meeting with the small group that was our church, about 20 people, and we were to celebrate the table of the Lord. When Sarita heard of it, she wanted to go. We tried to discourage her because of the weather and her delicate condition, but she was determined to go and would not accept "no" for an answer. We also did not want her to go because our youngest child, Daniela, was sick and my wife had to stay home to take care of her. But nothing worked. So I found myself driving with Sarita to the meeting, having covered her with as many layers of warm clothing as possible. Once in the meeting, Sarita wanted to participate; she wanted to partake of the bread and the wine as we celebrated the table of the Lord. When I looked at her, she had a glow around her, as she took part in the celebration – a very meaningful moment for her and her relationship with God.

Shortly after Sarita's third dose of chemotherapy, we decided that we would go back to Bolivia when her treatments were complete. But then one day she started feeling so unwell that we had to rush her to the hospital where she was admitted for care. In three weeks she was on life support; her lungs were not working well, then her kidneys started to have problems, and finally her liver gave up. The doctors told us that the time had come to make the hard decision to disconnect her from the life support systems.

My wife, Miriam, knew my heart was glued to my daughter's and that she had become the apple of my eye. So as things developed in the ICU room with nurses, doctors and other people hovering around, and me getting the hard news that compelled me, with great difficulty, to sign the authorization, Miriam went to the side of Sarita's bed and held her hands and then she spoke these words that I overheard:

"Sarita, today you will be in heaven with your brother and sister. I'm very concerned for your father's wellbeing; I do not think he will be able to bear the pain of losing you. Therefore I want to ask you one thing: as soon as you meet Jesus, I want you to ask Him to help your dad to be able to cope with your departure."

As I was in the midst of it all, hearing my wife speaking to my daughter in such a manner, it made me think my wife had lost touch with reality. How could she speak to our daughter like that? But I could do nothing as she already had spoken…

Three days later, we were standing beside what was going to be my daughter's grave in a cemetery in Laurel, Maryland. The funeral director left us to have a moment by ourselves, and as I was standing there with Miriam and my daughter Daniela, I began looking at a nice place close to a tree where we were to bury my Sarita. As we were meditating and praying, suddenly I started to see something in my mind.

In this vision, I was suspended in the air. To my right, there was a dirt road with people on both sides of the road as if ready to watch a parade; at the beginning of the street, there she was, my little Sarita, standing ready to walk towards the other end. She was dressed in a white dress and on her head she had leaves – olive and laurel – as the Olympic champions of the past used to wear; then I looked to my left and there were stairs that led to a great light at the end of them. I knew that light was God, and somehow I understood He had His arms open waiting to receive and reward my little Sarita; then I felt this joy in my heart that was so great, because I was seeing the entrance of my daughter to eternity, and God was waiting for her, and she was to be rewarded for her time on earth and how she blessed the heart of her parents.

I cannot describe with words the joy I felt, the certainty of the reality of what I was seeing in my spirit. It was a heavenly moment that God allowed me to experience and see, to comfort my heart from the terrible loss that I had experienced with the departure of my daughter, and to honor my wife's request to Sarita in her last moments on earth.

I understand that to certain people this could be taken as just the imagination of my heart, or a self-effort of my mind to make sense of the recent experiences and the departure of my daughter, but there is one more thing to it, and it is that my heart was completely healed from the pain of her departure. The joy and comfort that I experienced was so great that it healed all the pain and suffering that I had inside of me. This was no fabrication of my mind; this was not mere imagination.

Rather, I was granted access to the Eternal to see what was happening in the presence of God, and God used that to heal my heart and my wife's heart as well, because when I shared my experience with her, she told me that, although she could not see anything, she could sense in her spirit this joy and comfort that came from no human source, but from the Spirit of God Himself.

Two days later, we were preparing to celebrate my daughter's funeral, but we did not have a place or a church in which to hold a funeral service. We did not have money to rent a funeral home for visitation. So we had a very simple funeral service at the graveside of Sarita, over which I officiated. When I was speaking to the few people that attended, I saw Dr. Winkelstein from Johns Hopkins Hospital, one of the scientists that was in charge of Sarita's case while in the hospital. He was very kind and stayed to the end, and came over to us to present his words of kind support. As I thanked him I thought, how amazingly thoughtful of him to come. After expending a great deal of effort in helping with Sarita's treatment, he had no obligation to be there; he had fulfilled his duty while in the hospital, but yet there he was, attending my daughter's funeral.

This is another characteristic that I found in the Land of the Free and Home of the Brave: you can be very important and as well-educated as possible, but you can still keep that human touch that shows greatness of heart in all levels of society. As we were ready to close the service, I looked once again to the casket where Sarita was lying for her final rest; she was wearing the beautiful blue dress she had bought, with the fine white gloves that were included with the set.

She did not know, when she went to the mall with her mom, that she was choosing the dress she was going to wear in her own funeral.

As I observed this supernatural comfort that I felt in my heart was so real, I knew with absolute certainty she was alive in heaven. Sarita had obeyed her mother's request to seek special comfort for me... God allowed us to see into the Eternal, where a greater reality awaits us if we walk in His will.

Throughout the time of Sarita's treatment and before and after her passing, we found ourselves supported by wonderful people of all ethnicities: Latino, African American, Caucasian, Asian, Jewish, and people of all colors and backgrounds. In this we found one more characteristic of the Land of the Free and Home of the Brave: people in America gather to help when they see a need, and we received prayers and loving help from many of them.

A few weeks later, Miriam and I were getting ready to return to Bolivia. We had no more reason to stay, and we felt that everything in our lives was waiting for us back there in our own land. However, after praying and considering all factors, we began to feel from the Lord that there was something else we still needed to do in America and, with the blessing of the pastors and friends from back home, we concluded that it was best for us, with our daughter Daniela, to stay here as a family and to start anew.

It has been 18 years since Miriam and I arrived in this country – a land that now is ours...a land where we were so kindly accepted with open arms. We founded "Ekklesia USA," a Reston, VA church that is thriving. We meet every Sunday to serve Jesus by continuing the great American tradition of welcoming with open arms those in need as well as introducing Jesus to all who are in search of eternity in heaven. Many people, especially parents, can relate to the emotional anguish and the spiritual trials of losing their children. We documented our story in our testimonial book called *The Other Face of Victory* and on our website (ekkle.com), and have traveled to many countries sharing all that God has done in our lives. We are grateful that we have experienced our own American dream, which to us is the greatness of its people, the courage to fight, the sensitivity to help, the ability to remain human and the freedom to find faith, to worship, and to express our faith in the fullness of its reality.

May God bless America – The Land of the Free and Home of the Brave.

In 1973, while working alongside evangelist Julio Cesar Ruibal during the great revival in Bolivia, Carlos Penaloza was called into ministry, only months after his own conversion.

He studied at Portland Bible College, formerly called "Bible Temple" located in Portland, Oregon, and also received training at Leadership for Leaders in Haggai Institute of Singapore. He worked as a missionary in Colombia, at "Ekklesia Centro Cristiano Colombiano" and was the founder of "La Cominidad de Amor." Today it is known as "Mision Carismatica al Mundo," a church with a congregation of over 14,000 people.

He also established missionaries and churches as part of Ekklesia in Bolivia, Chile, Argentina, USA, Spain, Germany, the Middle East and other international locations.

Currently, he is the president of a missionary organization named "Cominha." He and his wife, Miriam, also founded and pastor "Ekklesia USA," one of the largest metropolitan Hispanic churches in the Washington, DC area. Pastor Carlos Peñaloza is a well-known international speaker and is known as the "The Job of the New Testament" because of his testimony written in his book The Other Face of Victory *that is currently available worldwide in both English and Spanish.*

JESUS, SAVING ONE GENERATION AND THE NEXT

John Cha

In the countryside of what is now North Korea, my father – Moon Jae Cha – was raised by his parents along with his four brothers. He was taught about Christianity ever since birth, but by his late teenage years, he had wandered away from the faith. He was overwrought by the heart-wrenching plight of his people and his country and by the miserable situation faced by his own family.

How could he and his family survive, he wondered? He was already drafted into the Imperial Japanese Army and now, out of desperation, he decided to throw his lot in with the occupying army. Placing his hope in military might and brute force, he enlisted as a young cadet officer in the Japanese army. Embittered by the daily discrimination he faced in the Japanese army and the desperate straits around him, he sought to get drunk and then in his drunkenness lashed out at the unsuspecting citizens and people of Pyong Yang. During his leave from the camp, he regularly drank heavily and terrorized local market places, even brandishing and using his military saber to demolish the market stalls. And then, on a fateful summer day in 1945, my father faced the darkest moment of his life. He received orders from the Japanese army to fight on the Russian front. No one had ever returned alive from the Russian front. My father knew he would never come back.

On the night before his deployment, he lay in his cot. Broken and tearful, my father reached back in his heart and mind to Jesus Christ and the Bible, which had become to him a distant memory. He remembered hearing, as a child, about a God who saved. And so, he prayed, "Jesus, if You save me from the front, if You rescue me right now, I will turn to You and will serve You for the rest of my life."

The next morning, the Japanese troops were sitting in the train station, waiting to be shipped out. Suddenly, over the loud speakers, the Emperor of Japan announced that the Japanese Empire and forces had surrendered to the enemy. All the troops remained silent in shock and disbelief. Everyone held the Emperor in deep veneration, worshiping him as divine, but now, he was announcing his surrender. And while all the other troops asked in bewilderment, "What next? What happens to our nation?" my father wept, and in his heart, he said to God, "Thank You! I give my life to You."

From that day on, my father lived His life for Jesus. His passion for God grew in several ways. First, he grew in his passion to tell people about Jesus. He went to the very market places where he had terrorized the people earlier as a drunk, angry military officer. Where he had previously clenched a bottle of liquor in one hand and a military saber in the other, he now came with a Bible. He pleaded with the people to turn away from sin and to give their lives to Jesus. Many who recognized him were shocked. They referred to him as "Saul" who had now become "Paul." He was a fervent evangelist. Second, he read the Bible and prayed with an insatiable desire, and as he grew to know the

Lord, he grew in his love and devotion to Him. Finally, he grew to love the church and to shepherd the people. In his early 20s, he served as a children's pastor at a church in Pyong Yang. At this time, however, the newly established communist government began to persecute all the churches. The newly established authorities were wary of any teaching that was outside of the state, and as a result, all the pastors faced persecution.

This was my father's real test. The officials arrested any pastor who would preach the Bible from the pulpit. At my father's church, when the senior pastor preached on a particular Sunday, within a few seconds, the officials at the entrance of the church marched in, arrested the pastor, dragged him out in front of the congregation, and canceled the service. The church leadership met and agreed – they would NOT be afraid of man. They wanted to live true and faithful to Jesus and remain shepherds of the flock. The following week, the associate pastor, seeing the police already waiting for him to preach, stood up, opened the Bible, and began to preach. He, too, was arrested. The elders then – one by one – preached on the following Sundays, and each of them – one by one – was arrested. Finally, my father, as the children's pastor, preached. He was arrested, imprisoned, interrogated, and beaten, and was told to renounce his faith, but he remained faithful to Jesus.

By the time he was released six months later, the churches were all being closed down, and he knew that he might be called back for interrogation. And so he escaped into the mountains and hills of North Korea, near the border. But he knew he had to find a way to leave North Korea. After a few months of living off the land, he sought a way to flee to South Korea.

Blessings from Jesus … A Church Family and a Bride

In 1951, my father took his suitcase, containing all his meager belongings, and crossed over from North Korea into South Korea. Looking back at the terrain of what would soon become North Korea, he considered the land that he had once regarded as his home. But ever since becoming a Christian, it had become hostile to him. As he crossed the checkpoint and entered South Korea, he left his land with the intention to return for his family. Little would he realize that he would not be able to return. The borders would soon close. He would no longer be able to see or contact his family members.

As he set out to begin a new life in South Korea, my dad experienced blessing after blessing. His first blessing came as he served as a pastor in several churches in Pusan and Seoul. Even though his parents and immediate family were no longer with him, he found spiritual fathers, mothers, brothers and sisters within the church. Many took him under their wings and mentored him. Others warmly received him as their brother. It was while growing with the church family in Pusan, seven years later, that he was introduced to a young woman named Yong Ha Kim. Actually, according to standards back then, they were both considered, at 32 and 30, to be on the older side when they got married.

My mother, who was also from North Korea, had been working as a nurse, and having been trained by Japanese doctors and nurses, she was looking at a bright professional future. But one night, her older sister told her that she had been "born again" through her faith in Jesus. My aunt shared the Gospel with my mother. Later, through a revival meeting, my mother came to know and trust in Jesus. She, too, told Him that she would give everything for Him.

And now, instead of being a successful nurse, she was marrying my dad, a pastor. Together, they would serve several churches in Pusan and in Seoul. And together, they would have kids ... many kids. Six, to be exact.

And being the very Biblical pastor that he was, our dad named us three sons after Jesus' disciples – Peter, James, and John. Likewise, he named his three daughters after the three flowers referenced in the Bible – Sharon, Rose, and Lily.

Once the last one of us was born, our parents immediately began to ask God for direction into the next chapter of our lives. The answer seemed clear: the United States.

In the US: Jesus Saves and Calls a Family

In 1972, our plane landed in Los Angeles and, as we settled into our new life in the States, my father immediately began to pray and prepare for a church plant for Korean immigrants in the area. Some first-generation Koreans began to gather together, and within that year, Hebron Presbyterian Church was established in downtown Los Angeles. Our father ministered to the church members by faithfully preaching, praying, and serving the congregation in various practical ways – helping new Korean immigrant families with licenses, visas, employment, utilities, rent payments, and so on.

From my earliest memories of Dad on his pastoral visitations, I often saw him enter people's homes with things, his Bible in his hands and a 50-lb. rice bag lugged over his shoulders. Throughout the years in Hebron, God blessed the congregation. Unfortunately, the salary for the pastor of a small immigrant church wasn't enough to support a family of eight. So Dad also worked as a full-time janitor, cleaning office buildings and hospitals. He served as a pastor during the day and as a janitor during the night. Our mom took up a side job sewing and tailoring.

While our parents were busy with ministry and work, we six children were simply trying to master the English language and adjust to a new culture. We had a tough time navigating through the streets and schoolyards of South Central LA. We faced a lot of discrimination, fights, and bullying, but in all this, we began to experience God's grace through His presence with our family.

Our home became a refuge for us. Home also became a place of ministry for our parents. Whether they realized it or not, they were beginning to raise and shape a generation of their own children who would be impacted by the message and life of Jesus. Our parents shaped us in two ways. First, we grew up having family devotionals every morning and every night. Together as a family, we sang a hymn, read a chapter from the Bible, and each of us took turns praying for others and for each other. As a family, through our daily mornings and evenings with God, we sensed His presence in our household as we grew through every season of life.

Secondly, our home became a place of seeing our parents' faith lived out. Because my father served with Korean immigrant churches that borrowed other church buildings, he never had his own office. And so his bedroom was his office and our home became his weekday ministry operations center. For sixteen years, this is where we saw our father's relationship with Jesus lived out—from his sermon preparation, to his prayer life, to his daily chores around the house (vacuuming and folding laundry), to his planning out all his visitations for many families in need, and occasionally sneaking a hug from my mom and planting an affectionate kiss.

Dad also proactively involved us in ministry. We met the families that he ministered to. We assisted in tutoring some of the recently immigrated Korean children, helping them with English and their schoolwork. Also, as our dad got older, he was no longer able to carry those 50-lb. rice bags up three flights of apartment stairs, and so the sons took up that role. Our mother was constantly in prayer for our family and for our church. She was the greatest source of counsel and encouragement for my dad, weathering the storms of life and ministry with him.

As decades passed, our parents grew older. Naturally, their physical bodies began to weaken and their activities slowed down, but their faith took root and their legacy was handed off as a baton in a race. It's here where we saw God at work in the generations through the years ahead.

In 1984, in his final ministry term, Dad planted a church in Arlington, VA, the Korean Orthodox Presbyterian Church (KOPC); he would serve out his remaining years with this congregation. In 1987, he was diagnosed with advanced-stage colon cancer. He passed away and went to be with the Lord in February 1988.

Mom remained steadfast in her walk with Jesus and with us. For the following 11 years, she woke up at 5 a.m. and prayed fervently and regularly for our family and for the church. Her life was filled richly with people and with ministry as she continued to make visitations.

Peter was the first to leave for college. He attended the University of Chicago where his heart was set on being admitted to pre-med. He wanted to be a successful doctor, but after failing his first chemistry exam, his world fell apart around him. He needed Jesus. Through a friend's invitation, he started to attend a Bible study hosted by Intervarsity Christian Fellowship. Overwhelmed by the life and fellowship of the Christians that he met there, Peter gave his life to Jesus.

After his seminary training, Peter became a staff worker with IVCF where he served for seven years. Afterwards, he planted and pastored a church in Chicago. Later, he became a teaching professor at Trinity Evangelical Divinity School and also sat on the Board of Trustees with IVCF. He and his wife, Phyllis, are now passing on their faith to their son, Nathaniel, who is serving with an inner-city non-profit group, and their daughter, Elaine, who is serving with IVCF on her campus at Northwestern University.

Sharon's life changed forever in her first year at college when she underwent a near-drowning incident. As the waves pulled her out into the ocean, she prayed what had become the all-too-familiar prayer for our family: "Jesus, save me! I want to live for you!" She was rescued, and from that moment on, she lived for Christ. She became involved with a campus fellowship at George Mason University, a Korean- speaking fellowship of Campus Crusade for Christ (KCCC). Throughout her life, Sharon has been passionate about evangelism and discipleship, telling people about Jesus and helping them grow in their relationship with Him.

We call her the "Navy SEAL" evangelist of our family, going to those places where we wouldn't set foot. Whether it be in the tough, seedy streets of New York City to preach to Korean gang members, or flying to India to share with the locals in impoverished areas, Sharon has evangelized and successfully led many to Christ. By God's grace, she wants to lead 100,000 people to Jesus! She currently serves as a youth pastor for a Chinese immigrant church and is actively raising disciples through an organization called the Joshua Project. She and her husband, Daniel, are raising their daughter and son, Joy and Danny. Joy wants to be a teacher on the mission field and Danny wants to be a doctor (or a pastor – still undecided) in the field.

James surrendered his life to Jesus at a church revival meeting in Virginia. He later attended Cornell University and joined the Navigators campus Bible study there where he grew in the Word. He worked and served at KOPC where he and his family made plans to be trained and equipped for missions. They served in the Central Asia region for 10 years. At one point, he was arrested and interrogated, but was eventually released. All of us siblings joked with him, "This is one time where you'd get locked up behind bars, and Mom and Dad would've been proud of you!" James and his wife, Faith, are raising their two sons and daughter, Joniel, Josiah, and Karis. All three have a heart for Central Asia and Russia. Joniel wants to minister through international politics, Josiah through medicine, and Karis remains "available" to what God has in store for her future.

Rose also gave her life to Christ through campus ministry at George Mason, and got involved with KCCC. Youth with a Mission deeply ministered to her and enlarged her heart for discipleship. She was also active in serving as a women's pastor and a youth pastor in several of the local churches in the DC area. Currently, she has set up a discipleship-focused spiritual formation program called Daniel Discipleship Training School. Her heart is for the emerging next generation.

Lily went to Eastern College where she received her degree and training in Christian Education. Ever since she was young, she had a growing heart for children and for children's ministries. She worked for 12 years as a public school teacher and also served for many years at KOPC as children's director and pastor. She is currently a consulting resource for children's ministries among smaller Korean immigrant churches.

As for me, I am serving out my years here at KOPC, now re-named Open Door Presbyterian Church. It is my 16th year serving on staff at what started as my father's church plant. We now have two congregations within our church—a Korean-speaking first-generation congregation and an English-speaking second-generation congregation. Together, we are raising the next generation of children and youth. We are a church family of over 3,000 people, seeking to grow in Jesus and to share Jesus with others – both locally and globally. Together with my wife, Leanne, we are still raising our three young children, David, Noah, and Hannah. We dream of God's future for them.

"Thank You, Jesus"

Looking back, I can only give thanks to Jesus.

Thank you, Jesus, for hearing the cry of my father – a desperate 19-year-old North Korean military man – who was about to fight on the Russian front. Thank You for turning this man, facing his own end, into someone who would rescue lives and souls for You.

Thank You for watching over him as he entered a new life in South Korea with nothing but a suitcase in his hands. If he could only have seen the eternal blessings that all the suitcases in the world would not be large enough to contain.

Thank You for a match made in heaven. There was no better fit for Dad than Mom, and vice versa. None of us kids would be here if it weren't for them, and more importantly, we wouldn't be who we are now if it weren't for them.

And thank You for being a God not only of *nations*—faithful in war-torn Pyong Yang and Seoul and LA and in DC—but also of *generations*, who is faithful in 1940, 1980, and now. Your loving kindness extends from one generation to the next.

Psalm 78:2b-7a (NIV)
I will open my mouth with a parable;
*   I will utter hidden things, things from of old—*
things we have heard and known,
*   things our ancestors have told us.*
We will not hide them from their descendants;
*   we will tell the next generation*
the praiseworthy deeds of the LORD,
*   his power, and the wonders he has done.*
He decreed statutes for Jacob
*   and established the law in Israel,*
which he commanded our ancestors
*   to teach their children,*
so the next generation would know them,
*   even the children yet to be born,*
*   and they in turn would tell their children.*
Then they would put their trust in God ...

John Cha currently serves as the lead pastor of the English-speaking congregation of Open Door Presbyterian Church in Herndon, Virginia, which serves a predominantly Asian American body of believers. Rev. Cha graduated from the University of Virginia and Regent College. He is married to Leanne, and together they are raising their three children, David, Noah, and Hannah.

A BRAND NEW FATHER
Norman Tate

Unfortunately, I did not grow up in a Christian home. My parents were an interesting couple. My mother was thirteen years older than my father and she was an introvert. My father – much younger and a little "out there" – loved being around people. Neither of them attended church, or thought it important that their family attend church. I remember how I used to watch kids my age getting dressed up in clothes that I did not have, and getting into their family vehicle, heading out to church. Somehow the expression on the children's faces was hard to read. While I thought they weren't exactly ecstatic about having to leave their homes so early on Sunday morning, there was something I sort of longed for about the way the whole family, as a team, carried out this weekly ritual together.

My father always worked hard. I don't remember a time when he did not have at least two jobs. Two full-time jobs! And as a result, we did not have our dad around very much. When weekends came, he would hang out in a local bar. He would drink, and he loved to dance. My mother was always at home with the children. This led to some interesting conversations when my father did come home. Sometimes they would argue until the wee hours of the morning.

These arguments did not diminish his drinking, and his continued imbibing influenced his decision-making. For example, he decided he wanted to become a prizefighter. He would fight at various venues on Friday nights for which he would receive twenty-five dollars and some of the worst beatings that I had ever witnessed. He would always report that he had won, and because we were so glad to have him home, we always believed him. After all, he was our dad, and we believed that he could do anything.

My father had a big heart and would help anyone – whether it was money, or helping a family move from one area to another. He always seemed to be available. It seemed to me that sharing a few beers would be his wages and he did not seem bothered by this at all. Everyone loved Norman, Sr.

Eventually, his personality led him into politics. Richard Daley, Sr. ruled the city of Chicago during the 1950s and 1960s. My dad became an Assistant Precinct Captain – a fancy title that recognized him as one of the "heavies" in the community, hired to make sure that the people voted Democrat. I was not proud of this at all. My mother would not allow us to talk about it in our home, and questions would not be responded to. Somehow children have a sixth sense that allows them to quickly determine which subjects are taboo.

Dad's next pursuit was bowling. He would spend several evenings a week in the bowling alley and there was no doubt he was very good at the sport. In fact, he was as close to being a professional bowler as an African-American man could come in the 1960s. He won many tournaments, and there were trophies all over our home. Then, yet another demon came home to roost. He began to gamble at the bowling alley. In some weeks, he would win four and five hundred dollars during a Friday night outing. But then there were some evenings that saw him lose his entire week's salary. It didn't seem to faze him at all. He would pick up his bowling equipment and whistle all the way home.

And many Fridays, he would not even come home.

How well I remember the continued arguments that would last into the early morning. I could hear all of the bad language and, of course, could smell the alcohol. Even at the advanced age that I have now reached, I still really dislike the smell of alcohol. Something had to change, but I had no idea how my family was ever going to become a real family like we would see on *Ozzie and Harriet*, and *Father Knows Best*. My father worked all of the time, and when he wasn't working he was doing something else, somewhere else.

The problems on the home front had devastating results. My sister, Carol, who was two years younger than I, was so brilliant in elementary school that she skipped two grade levels before the eighth grade. She began high school at the tender age of 12 but then found herself unable to cope with being the youngest student in every class. She had no peers and no friends to share the lunch table with. Before her 13th birthday, she had her first nervous breakdown.

Emotionally, she was on a roller coaster until she died in 1997. She could not keep a job, still did not trust people enough to have a real friend, and even separated herself from the rest of the family. There were times that she would not speak to anyone in our home for two and three weeks at a time.

Carol was in and out of the hospital continually. This family "problem" continued to snowball, as it took its toll on me. I began to stay home from school even on days that there was nothing wrong. I just didn't want to be around anyone, and I certainly didn't want to explain to every teacher why my homework had not been done.

My personal problems were just beginning. Because I was so behind in my class work, I began to act out in class. This resulted in detention after detention, and eventually expulsion from school. My friends became the other "bad boys" in the community. And my downhill slide resulted in my behavior becoming totally out of character. I was in trouble; our family was in trouble.

Twelve-step programs generally teach that people cannot be helped until they recognize that they need help. Our family did not believe we were dysfunctional. All the families in our area were "messed up" and we saw ourselves as no worse than all of the other families that we knew. Family arguments, fathers who drank too much, and children who were not doing well in school were the norm. *They* may have needed help, but our family? We didn't think so.

Not only could we not accept that there was something wrong, but also our knowledge of God was totally absent. While we did not attend church, few in our community attended church. There was no concern or yearning for a spiritual life and yet, sadly, that was what all of us needed.

In the Chicago area, there were multitudes of neighborhood bars. They were called taverns. The men in our area would gather in our local watering hole after work and drink and argue about everything from sports to politics. I guess the subject of fatherhood and what that meant never made the agenda.

My father was one of the ringleaders of the "Drinking Daddies." But in one afternoon, all of this would change. A Christian man by the name of George Brown witnessed to my dad as he walked past the tavern one day. Eventually this conversation would move to the inside of the club. Mr. Brown talked about a man named Jesus, who was the Son of God. This God loved all of the people of the world so much that He sent His Son to earth to die for our sins. By just asking Jesus to come into our lives, we could be forgiven of our sins and become brand new from the inside out.

My father had never heard anything like this. It intrigued him. Mr. Brown came over to our house on several occasions. I remember hearing my father and Mr. Brown talking about the Apostle Paul until the wee hours of the morning.

My father eventually gave his life to the Lord. He became as committed to Christ as he had been to the world. Rather than coming home with the smell of alcohol, he would come home with Christian friends and they would study the scriptures together. Then he began family devotions with us before he left for work. I was about eight years old at the time, and I witnessed that my father had become a completely different person. He was, as St. Paul described, "a new creature in Christ."

He joined a local church. He sought to enroll in Moody Bible Institute, though his application was rejected because he had been divorced earlier in his life. He went to the school and cried like a baby in the registrar's office. Thank God, they changed their minds and allowed him to attend.

He began to teach Sunday school and, as a result of studying music, he eventually became the Minister of Music at our church. Oh, yes, one last thing: I was there, along with the rest of our family, when the pastor baptized my father.

No one can convince me that God cannot change a life. I saw it happen for myself. Because of the power of Jesus Christ, I had a brand new Father!

In my freshman year in college, I felt my own calling from the Lord to ministry. At the time, I was studying at Kansas Baptist College at Ottawa University in Ottawa, Kansas. I was afraid of the pulpit, and couldn't see myself getting up in front of the congregation every Sunday and preaching a sermon, but I did think that perhaps I might serve as a director of education.

I finished up my Christian Education studies in the Washington, DC area at Washington Bible College of Lanham, MD, and then became the youth pastor at the First Baptist Church of DC, at the corner of New Hampshire and Randolph Streets in Northwest DC.

After about seven years, I moved on to pastoring a United Methodist Church on the Eastern Shore of Maryland. I had met my dear wife, Joyce, in a United Methodist Church. As the daughter of a pastor, she had been immersed in church all her life and thankfully sort of knew what to expect as a pastor's wife. She and I served on the Eastern Shore for three years before I became the Chaplain for the District of Columbia Department of Corrections in Lorton, VA. Unfortunately, the Lorton facility was closed in the 1990s, with the men being shipped all over the country, far from their families.

The Lord was good to us, however, and a few years prior to Lorton's closing, we were called to Heritage Fellowship Church in Reston, VA, where I still minister to this day. The church has been a blessing to my family and me as we have watched it grow over the years from about 250 members to over 900 families. It is an honor to pastor there. We just opened a new facility two years ago on Fox Mill Road in Reston. We try to meet the needs of young and old alike, having a service that includes a Christian contemporary style of worship with a band/orchestra, as well as an array of older style hymns. While we are largely an African American congregation, our desire is to reach out and reflect the diversity of the community around us, which we are beginning to see happen.

If I were to share any words of wisdom to young people wishing to serve the Lord, I would say to simply seek God's will as to where you should serve, and if you serve faithfully, God will take care of every one of your needs. Joyce and I raised four children and now have four grandchildren, and we have seen the Lord's provision, mercy and blessing upon us through all the years that we have been in service. It is easy for young people to become ambitious about their calling (we all start small, yet with big ambitions), but I would exhort each one to just be faithful where you are and God will take care of the rest.

The Reverend N. A. Tate, a native of Chicago, Illinois, is a graduate of the Washington Bible College of Lanham, Maryland, where he received a Bachelor of Arts Degree in Christian Education. His seminary studies were completed at the Howard University School of Divinity, where he received a Master of Arts in Religious Studies, and a Master of Divinity degree. His doctoral studies were completed at the United Theological Seminary in Dayton, Ohio.

While in seminary, Rev. Tate pastored churches in the Peninsula-Delaware Conference of the United Methodist Church. Since 1995, he has served as the Senior Pastor of the Heritage Fellowship Church in Reston, Virginia.

He is married to Joyce Thomas Tate, and together they have four children and four grandchildren.

SEASONS OF MY LIFE
Patricia Funderburk Ware

The first season of my life was dominated by my Grandma Alice and her husband, Granddaddy Heck. This elderly couple was not related to me by blood but were trusted neighbors and friends who lived three houses down from my parents, Paul and Bert Stevens, my sister, Vera, and me. They loved me from the first moment they saw me as an infant in my mom's arms. The only explanation I can surmise for their passion for me was that God gave it to them as a part of His ordained journey for that season of my life.

There were three things these beautiful people poured into me as their babysitting duties went from a few hours a week to almost every day and oftentimes overnight. First, they taught me to absolutely love being "Colored," the term most people used for African Americans during the 1950s when I spent so much time with them. Secondly, they exposed me to Jesus in a different way than I heard about Him in the churches I attended with my parents.

There was something very personal about how Grandma Alice talked about God. Even though Granddaddy Heck sometimes got drunk, I knew he loved me and Grandma and he was trying to serve

Jesus by "doing good as best he could." Third, they convinced me that God had a great plan for my life, and that I would be used to influence the lives of many, many people around the world for His glory. They never told me what that plan was. She said that only I could stop it from happening by rejecting Jesus as my Savior. Though I heard this over and over from the time I could walk around their little one- bedroom shotgun house, I did not understand that I was rejecting Jesus until years later.

Grandma was very light complexioned with long, straight hair. I, on the other hand, was dark brown with short, kinky hair. I remember, as if it were yesterday, how Grandma would sit on a little stool, give me her hair brush and let me brush through her silky hair.

With each stroke, she would tell me how beautiful my hair was— how God didn't just lay it on my head and leave it, but He took extra time to tightly curl each strand lovingly until it was like a crown of glory framing my beautiful face. She said He selected the richest, darkest clay to make my skin as he covered me with His love. He didn't just put a slit in my face and call it my mouth; He carefully used as much clay as He wanted to mold full, dancing lips the same way He took the time to give me the fullest nose in His design box that represented a lot of work on His part.

She also told me that she loved her skin color, nose, lips and hair because God chose to give them to her and He made all things beautiful. As a three- or four-year-old, I didn't really understand what she meant by this, but to this day, I absolutely remember the words. And as I grew, I began to understand and embrace what she was trying to tell me.

Now Grandma's concept of beauty was so very unusual for colored people during those years. It was a fact that the more Caucasian features you had, the more beautiful you were considered to be, and oftentimes the more privileges and advantages you were given, even by other Blacks. But the die was cast in me in more ways than one. Grandma taught me to see people the way God sees them, not the way man judges them.

The next God-orchestrated season of my life was primarily influenced by my dad and the church community in which he was immersed. My father, Paul, was very active in the church and my mother, Bert, would say that Paul and Pat were the "churchingest" people she knew. Every time the doors were opened, we were there! I was baptized at age 12 and counted it a blessing to participate in the foot- washing service during Holy Communion, a ritual my peers hated.

My sister and I were very active members of Sunday school, choirs, usher boards and anything else our parents could get us into. Along with that was memorizing entire chapters of the Bible to recite wherever there was an audience. It was a perfect foundation for the career I was to later have as a professional actress. I also learned organizational skills by watching my father function in the many leadership positions he held in the church. I realized that everyone who attended church was not necessarily there to serve God. There were some ungodly activities going on that adults didn't always know the kids were watching. God kept me from becoming cynical and walking away from the organized church. Grandma's training helped me to keep my eyes on the good and not stop being good because other people were doing bad things.

The season of growing up in Wilson, North Carolina, a small, segregated southern city, left me with vivid memories of two towns in one. The first is where I lived on the colored side of town. My parents were hard working, well-liked members of the community. Though they were not college graduates – in fact, my father never received his high school diploma – we lived on a beautiful street in a middle-class neighborhood, along with teachers and one of the few colored doctors in the city. Our home and lawn were "House and Garden" magazine beautiful. It came from a strong work ethic—taking pride in the things with which God blessed us—and from never letting racism or white people define us or limit how high we soared.

My parents did not allow us to blame white people's behavior for any failures we had. They always said God is bigger than any white man and it's God who keeps us from the snares of the enemy! The Negro community placed a great premium on education. Yes, we must fervently support the Civil Rights Movement, fight unjust laws, and become actively involved in the political arena. However, most African American adults knew that education, entrepreneurship, strong families and behaviors based on godly values would be the key to us living the American dream long term. Consequently, the village concept was alive and well in the place where I grew up. The village nurtured us, disciplined us, and pushed us to be three times better than the white students because we knew our race was a negative in the job market at large.

The other Wilson I knew was tainted with "White Only," "Colored Only" water fountains, rest rooms, restaurant entrances, etc. Until my high school years, the only up-close conversational relationships I had with a white person were on my grandfather's farm as white farm families harvested crops alongside Negro farm families. I watched them from afar when we shopped downtown or when my dad allowed my sister and me to wait for him in the back room of Ship and Shore, a white-only restaurant where he worked part-time as a waiter. Negro children were carefully schooled in the rules of etiquette when encountering a white person in public.

We knew that a misplaced word, "disrespectful" facial expression or accidental bump into one of them could cost us and our parents dearly. We also curiously watched them in TV shows that omitted the existence of a thriving, productive and wholesome Black community. This "White only" Wilson angered me but did not consume my thoughts or cause me great grief. It was my preoccupation with what was happening within the walls of my own home that proved to be a greater threat to my spiritual, emotional, physical and mental stability than any "White Only" sign or racial slur I encountered.

My mother and father were getting a divorce! I do know I tried even harder to be accepted to ease the pain I carried with me constantly because my father did not live with us. It set the stage for my deep compassion for young people growing up in single-parent households, and my passion to help rebuild the African American family.

My third season of life encompassed the turbulent teen years. By then I had learned to ease the pain by unwisely becoming inseparable from my overprotective, devoted, handsome, brilliant boyfriend. I also hid it under a cloak of academic and community accomplishments. But…because I was dark complexioned I was told that, even if I did my very best, there were doors that would be closed to me. But the doubters didn't stop me from trying really hard to develop all of my gifts and talents. As a result – and I know now that it was mostly because God was in control – many of my goals were achieved.

I did many things that were, indeed, often reserved for lighter-complexioned Negro girls. One of them included being the first Negro from my county to be accepted into the North Carolina Governor's

School for Gifted and Talented High School Juniors and Seniors. My talent was acting. When it was rumored that I was going to audition, some of the teachers and students in my school encouraged me not to audition in drama, but to seek an area in academics because I was too dark-skinned to be an actress. According to them, the only roles I would get would be for servants. However, I did audition and was accepted into the school. And while there, I was given starring roles! It was always a thrill for me to excel and to break free of any limitations others placed on me.

The fourth season began in senior high school when both my parents remarried to wonderful spouses. My stepparents taught me many godly lessons. My stepfather eventually taught me how to love unconditionally and my stepmother taught me how to love my husband. It was learned not so much through conversation, but through years of watching their behavior. My mother and father were both extraordinary people who were gifted beyond measure.

If my mother had been born to different parents during a different time, none who know her doubt that she could have easily been the CEO of a Fortune 500 company. She was a licensed practical nurse that set the standards high for the other Negro women in her world. Always immaculately dressed, charming, and watchful over her children like a mother bear and lioness combined, she was determined to have the best for us and for her extended family. Her commitment, sacrifice and hard work paid off in many ways.

My brother is a retired telecommunications engineer with a lovely, intact family. My sister is a retired PhD college professor and administrator, also with a lovely, intact family. My father was a community servant par excellence. Prior to his death in 1997, he received numerous awards for his tireless efforts. After his death, a street, scholarship fund, organization, building and lifetime achievement award were all named for him.

So why couldn't these two giants stay married? I think it was because each was fulfilling their own separate dream without involving the other one. Instead, they could have come together around one captivating, God-crafted dream, as He molded them into a loving, accomplished couple. Unfortunately, neither was willing to relinquish enough of his or her own dream to find the perfect place of unity between them. Of course, there were other unrevealed issues only they could articulate.

I was caught in the trap of choosing sides but learning how to cope. Keeping the peace between them and bringing harmony to potentially volatile situations was often left to "Sweet Patsy." That was ME. Another skill which served me well in years to come.

In 1967, the fifth season in my life journey continued as I began my freshman year at Hampton Institute, now Hampton University. Between the summer of my junior and senior high school years, I was accepted into the university's Summer Theatre program for high school students. The first day on the campus, I was hooked. Hampton is located at the tip of a peninsula that juts out into the James River, which flows into the Atlantic Ocean. The beauty of the campus, the poise of the students, the care and concern of the faculty and the rigorous academic curricula all won me over. Hampton was the only college to which I applied. There was none other for me.

Each of the four years spent on Hampton's campus brought an experience that profoundly influenced many of my future life decisions. During my freshman year, I was invited to a speech given by Tom Skinner, an African American evangelist who was unknown to me. What compelled me to go was the topic of his speech, "Black and Free." I, along with hundreds of other students, wanted to know how a Black person living in America could actually be free!

We were entrenched in the struggles of the Civil Rights and Black Power Movements. Rhetoric was heated, emotions were running high and I was swept away with the passion of it all. I loved the Movement because I thought that if we prevailed, Black people would finally begin to see ourselves as Grandma Alice said God saw us: beautifully and wonderfully made, physically and intellectually – the work of His own loving, just hands! When we did come to that realization, we would have more zeal to love and to please Him. At the same time, my anger had also turned on whites in a way that was counter to what I had been taught by my parents. I began blaming them for all of our problems as a people. There was a part of me that believed the only way to be free of the injustices of this nation was to "Burn, Baby Burn." So, yes, I wanted to hear where to set the next fire from this sought-after speaker, Mr. Tom Skinner, who was going to tell us how to be free… for real!

Tom had a "Grandma Alice surprise" for me. He told the audience that the only way for Black people or any person to be free on this earth and throughout eternity was through Jesus Christ, the only Redeemer of our souls. He shared the Gospel of Jesus' love and sacrifice for us…. all of us, regardless of our race. If Jesus loves us, how could we not first love Him and all of those He loves? When we surrender to Him, He actually comes to live within us so we can commune with Him moment by moment. I was enraptured by each word. Something clicked in me. I now know it was the Holy Spirit drawing me to Jesus.

My heart began to break for anyone, including white people, I considered my enemy. They needed Jesus' free gift of salvation as much as I did. I realized, after all of my years in church and years of listening to Grandma Alice, that I did not know the real Jesus of the Bible. I could recite scriptures about Him, but I did not have a deep love for, or personal relationship with Him. But I wanted it badly because I wanted to be free from hatred, anger, and rejection. I was tired of the struggle, of reaching for acceptance through worldly achievements. I wanted to know that Jesus knew me, heard my cries, understood my pain, wept over me as He wept over Jerusalem, rejoiced with me, and when I listened, talked to me in all the ways He talks to His own. After the speech my friend, Carl Ellis, asked if I wanted to accept Jesus as my personal Savior. I said "Yes!" before Carl finished his sentence.

The strangest thing happened. He stuttered, said I was making the right choice, and asked me to meet him at the same place the next evening so He could pray for me. Years later, I heard Carl speak in a message about the challenges of witnessing to African Americans during the turbulent 1960s. Jesus was referred to by many of us as "the white man's God" and African American Christians were often called "Uncle Toms." Consequently, he had gotten used to fervently defending his faith as an effective apologist. He needed some time to reflect on how to handle this eager young lady. Should he push her first to know everything he knew about Jesus before giving her life to Him, or should he believe the Holy Spirit had already done the work in her heart? I did return the next night and Carl lovingly led me through a prayer of repentance and acceptance of Jesus' gift of salvation! I was finally Black and Free!!!!

Now that the season of searching for my Savior was past and I knew Him as my Redeemer, the sixth season of my journey came quickly. Standing on the steps of Ogden Hall on Hampton's campus during the second semester of my freshman year, I wailed in agony along with others after hearing the news of Dr. Martin Luther King's assassination. That moment in time began my relentless journey of seeking justice, redemption and empowerment for my people. I became an outspoken student political activist.

Years later, that little taste of politics evolved into political appointments in the administrations of two U.S. presidents and personal interaction with political figures around the world. Throughout my career, I have developed local, state and national organizations to address these issues. As a Christian, I was acutely aware that everything I did had to be directed by the Holy Spirit. Even if I did not mention the name of Jesus, the core values of all of my work had to be those in agreement with His Word.

During my sophomore year, I was ecstatic when one of the African Diaspora students spent Thanksgiving in North Carolina with my family and me. The seeds of love for Africa that grew out of that friendship led to involvement in humanitarian and corporate projects in Africa and to serving as a consultant for youth leaders in many independent African nations.

As a speech and drama major, I represented the department as Miss Hampton Players during my junior year. Long, grueling hours spent in the C. C. Armstrong Building with the greatest drama professors on earth, helped prepare me to receive a Master of Fine Arts degree in speech and drama; perform in a cross-country and world tour; and appear in TV and radio commercials, industrial films and an Academy Award-nominated film.

The summer before my senior year, Hampton sent me to Sweden as a student ambassador. It ignited a passion for travel and a love for people of all races, ethnic groups and cultures. Prior to this experience, I had a fear of travelling to other nations because I did not know how I would be received as a Black person. I was so accustomed to being thought of as a second-class citizen here in the U.S. that I didn't know if it would be the same in other countries. I was treated with extraordinary love, respect and care by the Swedish family with whom I lived that summer and by the Swedish people in general. God used the Sweden adventure to take the fear of traveling to other lands from me.

He knew the plans He had for me, including being a world traveler and influencer of people globally, just like Grandma and Granddaddy Heck told me over a half century ago. I also learned that, beneath the skin, all of His people are the same. Our differences come mostly from cultural diversities and experiences; but the hearts, molded by God the Creator, have the same potential for good and for evil. We are all seeking to fill a place in it that God reserved only for Himself. I've seen this up close and personal while traveling to nearly 50 nations.

My seventh season came during my senior year at Hampton when I married a fellow student. A part of the decision came from the fact that I was still, in essence, a baby Christian, not knowing how to truly discern the voice of God as weighed against His Word and godly council. The other part was that I still had deep wounds from my parents' divorce and was still subconsciously looking for acceptance and stability; I married for all the wrong reasons.

That marriage afforded me the opportunity to be a military officer's wife and to live and work in Seoul, South Korea. But…another wound to the soul!. After several years, the marriage ended in divorce. The pain of the failed marriage and challenges of being a single parent to our beautiful daughter, Eboni, added fuel to my passion in later years to help strengthen and rebuild the African American family and to focus on youth development issues.

During this season of emotional, physical and spiritual struggles, God led me to resign from my job, sell my home and move into one of the economically depressed areas in my city. This was unparalleled preparation for later years of advocating for the poor and underserved! I lived with their distress, felt it, was overcome by it and defeated it. The destructive life styles all around me became traps that were deceptive in their empty promises of freedom. Like the sobering, unforgettable words of single moms in my building unit and in the adjacent housing projects: "When life seems so hopeless, you do whatever you can to ease the pain for a minute, an hour, a few days… knowing that it will return. But many of us wrongly believed we had to have those fake 'highs' to survive."

With God's guidance, we, the people, found ways to be overcomers and get clean of the short-term fixes. With determination, courage and faith, we created a Community Development Corporation that helped residents start businesses, rebuild families, become home owners, and more. My neighbors, who once were wallowing in pity, hopelessness and helplessness, were beginning to look like my parents' generation. They not only survived, but thrived in many ways the oppressor never thought possible. After four amazing years of growth in my faith and learning lessons of trust, humility and obedience, Eboni and I left that wonderful community to begin another season in the journey of life.

In Biblical terms, the number eight represents "a new beginning." It was in the eighth season of my life that God truly did a new thing with me. I began my journey in the national political arena and, after twenty years of being a single mom, I met and married the most wonderful,

"Jesus-follower" of a man, Bradley Richard Ware. Brad has brought stability, unconditional love and godly leadership into our lives as we have traveled these past two decades together as one in Christ. He now has a thriving medical practice in which I am involved, along with my continued development work in the U.S. and internationally. To our great joy, we are also proud, doting grandparents to Eboni's two adorable daughters, Leylah and Zoe.

The theme of this current and ninth season of my life is "Pass It On!" God has given me an awesome satellite view of my life up to this point. Tears, triumphs, joys, failures, sins, surrenders, etc. are like little signposts strategically strewn along the mapped-out trail of my journey.

What next, my Father? God has said we are not to leave this earth without having equipped the next generation of His people with what He has placed in our hands…we must "Pass It On!"

Oh, God, our God… I will be obedient and bless your people, as You direct… and as You have blessed me through the many turbulent, triumphant, grace-filled SEASONS of our lives.

Patricia Funderburk Ware is President and CEO of The Ware Development Group, Inc., specializing in media/ entertainment, health, community revitalization and youth development. She has performed as a professional actress throughout the U.S. and globally; trained future leaders in the U.S. and internationally; served as a political appointee and/or adviser in five U.S. Presidential Administrations; appointed as a Goodwill Ambassador for UNESCO Center for Peace; and lived in South Korea and Sweden.

A few of her many awards include The Order of the Long Leaf Pine, North Carolina's highest community service award; Hampton University's 20th Year Outstanding Alumni Award; and the African Diaspora Development Award.

She has a BA from Hampton University, MFA from The Catholic University of America and an Honorary Doctorate of Letters from Aspen College.

Mrs. Ware and her husband, Dr. Bradley Ware, a Family Practice physician, live in the Washington, DC area. Their daughter, Eboni, a Hampton University graduate, is an executive in the music recording industry and lives with her family in Spring Hill, Tennessee.

MY JOURNEY
Sam Sadek

I was born in December 1971, in the city of Al-Minya in southern Egypt. Al-Minya lies about 150 miles south of Cairo, the capital, which is located on the banks of the Nile River. Cairo is famous for its many tourist attractions, including temples and museums that contain thousands of ancient Egyptian archaeological pieces dating back thousands of years to the time of the Pharaohs. There are also many ancient churches and monasteries dating back to the first century AD, when Christianity was introduced to Egypt.

I was born into a religious Coptic Orthodox family to Egyptian parents, and was raised as a Copt. I was baptized with water as a child according to the Coptic tradition.

My father, a devoutly religious Copt, worked as a traveling wholesale merchant. He was often invited by a Christian neighbor to go with him to the church where he used to worship. But every time, my father would strongly reject the invitation, telling him he was Coptic and had no desire to go to those Protestant churches. According to his reasoning, the Coptic Church was the original and "Mother Church."

And sometimes my father would come up with excuses to avoid going to church at all, such as life concerns, issues related to his work, and the demands of his trade, which caused him to be away from the area.

One day, however, my father entered the house and his face was different. When my mother asked about his condition and where he had been, he told her he had gone with his friend to attend a worship service at one of those Protestant churches on the other side of the city. He told her that during the service and the last prayer, he had a strange feeling he had never felt before. He told her that during prayer he felt a heavy burden in his heart, like a load on his shoulder. He prayed earnestly, with tears, asking God to forgive his sins and to save him from this condition, and after this prayer, he felt very peaceful in his heart and soul!

My father passed away in 1979 at the age of 40. He had undergone surgery, and an infected wound had caused poisoning to his system. My father left behind him a family consisting of seven members – six children between the ages of four and seventeen, and my widowed mother.

Even though my mother was only 35 years old and under lots of pressure from others, she refused to remarry or to send her five young children to a children's orphanage in another city to raise us up. She insisted on devoting the rest of her life to raising us. And in addition to that huge responsibility, for the first time in her life, my mother had to go out and work.

She endured great hardship and suffered a lot, day and night, in the cold and hot weather, as she worked in a simple grocery store close to the house, which often had nothing but some empty shelves. My father had not left us anything, but rather had accumulated debts due to his sickness and his inability to work in his final months.

I remember our life was extremely difficult. Even as an 11-year-old child, I used to work during the summer school vacation, taking on daily jobs to support my family. The work was very hectic for a child my age. It was also very risky and scary, as I faced danger on a daily basis. One summer evening in 1983, while I was working in the city market, a driver tried to kidnap me, but I was able to escape and run away.

Though we attended church, I have no recollection of us having any family prayer time or Bible reading together. Prayer for us was limited to the congregational prayers, which were usually written in a small booklet that we used at church.

From the ages of seven to eleven, I used to help the priest in conducting the mass as an altar boy, where I learnt the melodies and the refrains in the old Coptic language.

In the summer of 1982, my mother was invited by my brother's friend to attend a revival meeting at one of the local Protestant churches. When my mother arrived at the church and saw how it looked on the inside, she realized this was the same place where my father had attended a few years earlier, where he had given his life to Christ!

The meeting was a strange experience for my mother, since she was not used to this kind of worship. As the preaching began, she felt the sermon was directed to her personally and that the Lord was revealing all her thoughts. My mother kept going to the evening meetings and, through the prayers and preaching of the Word of God every night, she was deeply touched. This verse had a profound impact on her:

"For by grace you have been saved through faith. And this is not your own doing; it is the gift of God, not a result of works, so that no one may boast." (Ephesians 2:8, 9 ESV)

She understood she could not go to heaven based on her good works, by being a good person or by keeping certain traditions or practicing religious rituals, but rather by putting her faith in Christ alone. She also discovered that a person could know and be assured of his salvation in the here and now.

This was a very strange thing for my mother, as she was brought up according to the Coptic Orthodox church's teachings, where the person had to try and work hard to receive salvation and to enter heaven based on his good deeds in his life before God. The deeds were basically her main reason for attending church regularly, for praying to God and to the saints, reading the Bible, and giving to the church and to the poor.

She felt that no matter how spiritual a person might be, they could not have assurance of going to heaven. This was considered pride or deception from the devil. Throughout her life, what my mother heard was that a person could never know where he would spend his eternal life until his death and his resurrection on the judgment day, when God would bring each one's deeds and weigh them on a scale and then decide whether a person would enter heaven or hell.

Then my mother heard the message of the Gospel and the teachings regarding the new birth and eternal life through belief in Jesus. She heard John 3:16 for the first time in her life:

"For God so loved the world that he gave his only begotten Son, that whosoever believeth in him should not perish, but have everlasting life." (KJV)

The Lord opened her heart to know that the only way to receive eternal salvation was by realizing she was a sinner and that only by the salvation of Jesus could she be saved from the punishment and judgment of God; she could not be saved by her own good works. But by coming to God and repenting of her sins and believing with all of her heart that the Lord Jesus Christ had died for her on the cross of Calvary and rose from the dead to pay for all of her past, present and future sins, she understood, with deep conviction and faith, that she could receive a new life and a new nature; also, the Holy Spirit would come and dwell in her repentant heart forever. She was able to understand that, in this way, she was set free from the slavery of sin and would escape the punishment and judgment of God. She was assured of going to heaven based upon the atoning work of Christ.

And so it happened that at one of those evening meetings, my mother confessed her sins and asked God to forgive and accept her as His redeemed child. That night my mother became a new creature in Christ and her life changed completely.

My mother told my older brother what had happened to her and how the Lord had changed her life, but my brother was skeptical and did not believe her words. He also refused my mother's continuous invitations to go to the meetings. My mother prayed fervently for him that he would come and hear the Gospel so he would not perish, hoping that the Lord would open his heart and he would accept the free salvation presented to him in the Lord Jesus Christ the Savior.

A few weeks later, my brother decided to go and see for himself! When my mother saw him there, she was surprised and thanked the Lord. And she started praying immediately that the Lord would speak clearly to his heart.

The Holy Spirit was present in the place and he started to feel disturbance in his soul. The Lord spoke to him in a very clear way and brought to mind all the sins that he had committed so that he felt a strong conviction. At the end of the service, the preacher gave the invitation and, without any hesitation, my brother walked to the front and prayed, crying out to God to save him from the slavery of sin which had shackled his life, and especially from the habit of smoking cigarettes, which he had done from a very young age.

That night my brother completely changed. He enjoyed the Lord's peace, which the Holy Spirit gave him and which abided in his heart from that point onward. His life and behavior completely changed and this astonished everyone around him. He became a witness of the grace of God that had completely transformed his life.

He faithfully served the Lord, with humility and devotion, until the day he went to be with the Lord at the age of 28 years, after suffering for a few days from a sudden, severe illness. It was such a shock to my mother and to us children, to our relatives, acquaintances and all believers who knew him well.

Following my mother receiving salvation and new life in Christ, and my older brother's salvation, my two older sisters also received the grace of salvation.

During those days, I remembered feeling I had been given a new family, so different from the one I had known weeks and months before.

Their lives, words and behavior had changed in an amazing way! Our house became a church! Families and individuals would visit our house. Bible studies and prayer meetings were held there on a regular basis.

Despite those great spiritual blessings that we enjoyed, and the new spiritual family of which we were members, our life was not free from opposition, harassment, and persecution. In fact, we experienced satanic attack in many different ways.

The amazing thing is that the Lord used this affliction and opposition to strengthen our faith and to shape our spiritual life so that we became more like Him. And even some of the hard people who had come against us came to know Christ personally and received eternal life, becoming members of our heavenly family.

When I was 11 years old, I started going with my mother and siblings to the evening meetings at the new church. I started to participate in the children's church activities and the church became an integral part of my life.

One summer day in 1983, I went to the Sunday school at church. Most of the attendees were younger children and there was only one class for all ages. I felt bored, so I left the church and started walking down the street until I reached the intersection of a side street where something caught my attention! I heard children singing with a loud sound – songs that I knew. The voices were coming out of a big building with high windows! I followed the sound until I came to the main entrance of the building, which I discovered later was a Protestant church. So I crept into a small door next to the main church entrance. This door led to a long hallway which ended at another hallway that led to the church back entry doors. I crept in with great anticipation.

I stopped when I saw a small square glass display at the edge of the back hallway.

What got my attention was a complete copy of the Bible. Underneath it was written "40 weeks." When I looked at the rest of the displayed items, I found different things such as a pen, a box of crayons, a notebook and a New Testament. At that moment, I was surprised by a man behind me who asked, "Are you looking for something or someone specific?"

I got scared for a minute and told him, "No, I am new here and I entered because I heard the sound of the songs from the outside. I don't know anything about this place." Then he asked if I wanted to attend the class designated for my age group. I told him, "I will."

Before I left him, I asked him about the secret of those items displayed in the display case and the significance of the number of weeks. I learned from him that I could receive this Bible if I attended and completed a 40-week special program.

Instantly, I decided in my heart and soul to own this Bible no matter how much it cost me! I was counting the days and the weeks and dreaming of the day when I would receive my own personal, complete Bible with my name written on it.

I started attending the Sunday school every week and I found I had a strong desire for the written knowledge of the Word. I was so eager to listen to the Bible stories, particularly those of the Old Testament.

One of the events that had a huge influence on my spiritual life and helped me to learn and memorize the Word of God was "Vacation Bible School," which was held at the church for ten consecutive days, lasting four hours daily. There were many different activities that were beneficial and interesting for all ages and I thoroughly enjoyed it.

Days, weeks and months passed by and the promised day came, which I will never forget. It was the day I received the full Bible. I will never forget how it felt to own a Holy Bible, just for ME! I felt very wealthy, extremely happy and I could almost fly with joy, as if I owned everything in the world! The Bible became my sole, intimate friend that has never left me since that time!

When I turned thirteen, I stopped attending the children's Sunday school. I joined the youth meeting at the church for those from the ages of thirteen to seventeen. In the summer of 1984, I went to the youth summer camp with a group from the church. I was so excited since it was the first time in my life to experience riding a train and traveling to another city! The camp was full of young teens from all the various regions of Egypt.

I remembered the many useful activities that were held during the summer camp program, including the different workshops, Bible studies and competitions! I particularly loved the new songs we were taught. I was also intrigued and deeply moved by the theater and drama which was presented to us on the last evening.

We met outside at the campground after dinner in a huge green meadow, with many chairs placed in the shape of a circle to accommodate all the participants. The evening started with singing and then the drama began. The setting was in a police station where a sheriff sat in his office and a young officer stood nearby, guarding the station.

After a few minutes of the Sheriff talking to the young policeman, many people started coming to the police station, one after another, and they all had similar stories. They came to report the sudden disappearance of a family member, relative or acquaintance. They were all very perplexed and did not know the reason behind the disappearance of those people who were of different ages, backgrounds and social classes from the same village.

The testimony was consistent among all those family members speaking about the missing individuals. They were good people, had no enemies, hatred or problems with anyone that might have caused either their being kidnapped or anyone taking revenge against them. At the same time, the police station phone started ringing, with many other people calling in to report the disappearance of their relatives with similar stories!

Signs of fear and confusion started to appear on the face of the officer in charge, who seemed to think that there was a large gang of criminals who had gathered together and agreed to the simultaneous kidnapping of a number of residents of the village. I remembered that I was very astonished and confused, trying to guess what could have happened to those people.

As they were talking, screaming and exchanging different scenarios that could have happened, a person dressed in a suit and holding the Bible came to the police station. This person came to report the disappearance of his young and only son. He instantly learned from the other people gathered there that they had also come to report the exact same thing regarding their loved ones!

The man was very surprised, but after a few minutes of astonishment and sadness that fell on the room where they were meeting, he started screaming loudly, remorse and anguish on his face: "I think I know exactly what happened to those people!"

Everyone, including the sheriff, asked him: "What are you saying? What is your job? And how do you know what happened to all those different people?"

Then the man told everyone he was a pastor and he knew the reason behind the disappearance of all the missing people because it was predicted in the Bible. Everyone was astonished and very curious to know what was behind the matter.

The pastor started to tell them: "I knew I was not a true believer!!"

He read some verses and parts of the Bible and told them that this event that had occurred was called the "Rapture". It meant that Christ came and took all the true believers who received salvation through His Grace to heaven and He left the rest here to face pain, suffering, oppression and death!

When I listened to the screams of those people and saw how confused they were, I felt very scared and my heart was beating very quickly. I imagined that this event had actually occurred, and thought in my heart: Was there any hope for those people left behind? Due to the fear and horror, I was holding very tightly to the chair I was sitting on! Soon there was no one left in the scene except this pastor, who started talking to us as youth about the eternal and the second coming of Christ.

In a few moments, he presented a wonderful and strong message of salvation. He told us: "Today, if you are not sure of your salvation and whether you are going to heaven, you have a golden chance to open your heart, admit your sins and repent. You can ask Christ to come into your heart to save you from all your sins and to give you a new life and a new heart and to write your name in the Book of Life. Then you will be assured that you will spend your eternal life with Christ in heaven!!"

Those words were like a lifeline "rescue," offered to someone drowning, or like cold water for a thirsty soul, ready to die in a dry desert! At the end of the gathering, the preacher offered an invitation for the ones who were willing to give their life to Christ – to accept Jesus as their personal Lord and Savior.

During the invitation hymn that included words of salvation and a heavenly eternity, I got out of my place and proceeded to the front with the many others who went forward, and I prayed, confessing that I was a sinner. I gave my life to Christ the Savior and asked him to come and save me and write my name in the Book of Life. I felt complete peace and joy in my heart after the meeting. Something had happened inside of me that I could not explain! The next day I went back to my home city.

I began to feel the presence of God in my life in a way I had never felt. I also had a strong desire to please God and to obey Him in all possible ways and in all areas of my life. I had feelings of sadness and fear, however, when I would fall into sin. Sometimes, when I sinned, I felt the Lord Jesus was so displeased with me that He left me, I was no longer His son, and that I lost my salvation.

But I learned from reading the Bible, and especially from certain verses of Scripture, that there was a difference in the life of a true believer regarding our relationship and fellowship with God. When I accepted Christ as my Savior and Lord, I became a son of God, and accordingly, I became a member of God's spiritual family. God became my Father and He will never disown me, no matter what I have done!

These verses were of particular help to my understanding of God's grace and steadfast salvation for me:

John 1:12 "But to all who did receive him, who believed in his name, he gave the right to become children of God." (ESV)

John 10:27-29 "My sheep hear my voice, and I know them, and they follow me. I give them eternal life, and they will never perish, and no one will snatch them out of my hand. My Father, who has given them to me, is greater than all, and no one is able to snatch them out of the Father's hand." (ESV)

As time went by, I grew more and more in my spiritual life and in fellowship with God, through prayer, reading and studying the Word of God daily, and through attending spiritual meetings and sharing fellowship with other believers.

God used His Word and also the guidance of many spiritual believers around me, despite the challenges and difficulties of life, to mold my life and personality.

As the years went by, I had a strong desire growing in my heart to serve the Lord. When I was 17 years old, I began leading several ministries at church and continued to do so in subsequent stages of my life. I also ministered in remote villages that were deprived of having a full time minister.

In the summer of 1990, following the death of my older brother, my health began to fail due to a life-threatening heart condition that had developed when I was a child. After consulting with some cardiologists and heart surgeons, they decided that I needed to undergo open-heart surgery to fix the problem. Having such surgery done in Egypt in those days was a great challenge, both medically and financially. But by God's providence and grace, I was able to have the procedure done in the winter of 1991, without any complications.

The Lord spared my life from certain death and gave me a new physical life and I was so grateful to Him. As a result of this incident, I vowed to the Lord to serve Him for the rest of my life, according to His will.

In the months that followed my surgery, I began to see the Lord guiding my steps toward a full- time ministry. During my third year in college, I was introduced to an American Christian organization called Campus Crusade for Christ, now known by the name CRU. This organization serves among college students all over the world.

Soon I began to be active in evangelism and discipleship ministry on my college campus. The fruit of that ministry was the birth of a weekly worship meeting for college students, held at one of the local churches in the area. The Lord was really at work on the college campus and dormitories and blessed those early days greatly!

In January 1993, I attended the CRU annual missions conference, which was held in a conference center in the city of Alexandria, Egypt. During the conference, through the preaching and teaching of the American missionaries about the Great Commission and God's personal calling to each person, I began to feel that the Lord was calling me strongly and clearly to the mission field. At the end of the conference, I prayed and promised the Lord I would devote my life to serving Him after I finished my college studies.

I graduated in May 1993 and the same month joined Campus Crusade for Christ. I spent close to six years in preaching ministry among college students, discipling hundreds and training leaders among them. Those were the most wonderful years of my life. The Lord blessed those years of service in an amazing way. During this period I experienced much fruit in my ministry, with many souls asking for salvation and receiving new life in Christ. College students were discipled, some were called to the mission field, and some dedicated their lives entirely to ministry.

In February 1999, the Lord opened a door to travel to the United States. There I joined a Bible college in the state of Ohio and in 2001 received a Master's Degree in Biblical Studies. I served as a preacher and pastor in an Arab congregation in the state of New Jersey and the city of Philadelphia. In October 2002, I moved to Washington, DC, the capital of the United States, and served as an associate pastor for four years in the Arabic Baptist church for that area.

Between the years of 2006 and 2008, I served in different ministries among various American churches. This included preaching at mission conferences in different states, and also teaching at one of the Bible institutes in Northern Virginia.

In February 2008, I returned back to pastoring among Arabic-speaking people. I moved to Manassas, Virginia where I currently serve as a pastor for the Arabic Baptist Church of Manassas, where we are reaching Arabs throughout the Washington, DC area with the message of the Gospel of Jesus Christ.

Sam was born to an Eastern Coptic Orthodox family in Southern Egypt. He came to know the Lord as his personal Savior in 1984 during a Teen Summer Camp in Southern Egypt.

After graduating from the University of Cairo with a BA in Social Work, Sam was called to become a full-time missionary with Campus Crusade For Christ (CRU) from 1993-1999. In 1999, the Lord opened the door for Sam to attend Marietta Bible Seminary in Ohio where he graduated with a Masters in Biblical Studies in 2001.

He then began serving among the Arabic-speaking communities in New Jersey, New York and the Philadelphia area. He served as Associate Pastor of the Arabic Baptist Church in Washington, DC from 2002 to 2006. From 2006-2008, Pastor Sadek traveled extensively, teaching on the subject of evangelism.

In 2008, Pastor Sadek became the pastor of Grace Church in Manassas, Virginia. In 2014, he also co-founded Revival Church in Sterling, Virginia, where he serves as a Senior Pastor, in this ministry to the Arabic Community of the greater Washington, DC area.

FINDING YESHUA THE MESSIAH
Neal Surasky

Unity. In Hebrew, the concept is represented by the word אֶחָד *echād*. In the Greek, it is represented by the word εἰς *hace*. They both mean "one." And in either language, it is a concept that is very Jewish. The solidarity among the Jewish people goes way back in our history – to when it wasn't so popular to be Jewish. Even today, the Jews will stick together when confronted by threats from outside. The proverbial circling the wagons is familiar among my people.

Growing up Jewish, it was an unspoken and understood fact that there was only one thing that could stop me being Jewish. And that was to be avoided at all costs. Of course, that was believing in Jesus. Even today, Jewish people are told that, once you accept Jesus as the promised Messiah of Israel, you are no longer Jewish. All you have to do is remember back to the movie "Fiddler on the Roof" and you will know what I mean. Tevye just couldn't accept his daughter Chava marrying a Fyedka, a non-Jew. Why? Because it was seen as a threat to the continued existence of the Jewish people.

While far from orthodox, I definitely had a Jewish identity. From a very young age, I can remember celebrating the Passover at two different relatives' homes, playing the game of finding the hidden *matzah*, and having great family time together. I can remember going to Hebrew school for about two years before my *Bar Mitzvah*, the Jewish ceremony that marks a young boy's passage into adulthood. Yet after the *Bar Mitzvah*, I never stepped foot back into the synagogue. At least not until I found the Messiah, Jesus. Ironically, even though Jesus is seen to be the one thing that will separate someone from Judaism, He was actually the one who brought me back to my Jewish roots.

You might wonder that I should say "back to my Jewish roots." Apart from my culture, Judaism had little or no spiritual meaning or significance until I came to faith. In fact, it was overcoming my ignorance of the Hebrew Bible that finally showed me who Jesus is, and that He was not just for my Gentile friends, He was for me.

I thought I knew who Jesus was when I was growing up. I "knew" that He wasn't Jewish, and didn't have anything to do with the Jewish people. In fact, I also knew that many who claimed to be followers of Jesus didn't particularly care for the Jewish people. So how could He be for me? And most importantly, I also "knew" that Jesus was found in the New Testament, and my Bible, the Old Testament, didn't mention anything about Him. Then my world was changed.

I was a very determined teenager, but not what I would call popular. I had a few friends, but my phone wasn't ringing off the hook with invitations to things. By the end of my junior year in high school, I had already decided where I wanted to go to college. So I applied early and was accepted to Penn State. And that was that. No other applications were needed.

In January of my senior year of high school, I was working at a bridge tournament. The other kids I was working with were all surprisingly from Penn State University, where I would be attending that fall. (For the record, I thought it was completely coincidental back then, but I have come to understand that there is no such thing as coincidence, a philosophy that I have come to call anti-coincidental theology!) Between the afternoon session and the evening session of the tournament, there was a break for dinner. These college students invited me to a Bible study that they were having during the break.

I cannot stress enough that it wasn't the fact that they were having a Bible study that was important to me. Neither was it a curiosity about the Bible. It had zero to do with spirituality. These guys went to Penn State! That's where I was going! And it was very important to me that they accepted me. I didn't get asked to go to a lot of things. So when they asked me, of course I agreed.

I don't think that, prior to that day, I had ever owned a Bible. So it should surprise nobody that I didn't bring one with me. I just sat at the table in that hotel room and listened as they read. And here is what they read.

> "Who has believed our message? And to whom has the arm of the Lord been revealed? For He grew up before Him like a tender shoot, and like a root out of parched ground; He has no stately form or majesty that we should look upon Him, nor appearance that we should be attracted to Him. He was despised and forsaken of men, a man of sorrow and acquainted with grief; and like one from whom men hide their face He was despised, and we did not esteem Him. Surely our griefs He Himself bore, and our sorrows He carried; yet we ourselves esteemed Him stricken, smitten of God, and afflicted. But He was pierced through for our transgressions, He was crushed for our iniquities; the chastening for our well-being fell upon Him, and by His scourging we are healed."

They continued reading, but at this point, I started to fade out a little bit. You see, I had a problem. It was very important to me that they accepted me. But I was Jewish, and they were talking about Jesus, something that I just wasn't supposed to do. And besides, they were reading from the New Testament, a book that I didn't believe in. What to do, what to do?

I quietly stood up and began to make my way slowly toward the door. Someone saw me and asked me where I was going. I tried to be as tactful as I could, and simply told them that I needed to go, and that I would see them after dinner. Someone asked, "Why are you leaving?" Again, trying to be as inoffensive as possible, I replied, "Look, you guys know I'm Jewish, and I don't believe in the New Testament, so I'm going to go, and I will see you after dinner. Enjoy the rest of your study."

The response to my statement, frankly, surprised me. Another question. "Wait. Why do you think this is the New Testament?" At this point, my pride kicked in. I have always been a logical person. Smart. Top of my class. And now my intelligence was being insulted. I told them that I knew who they were reading about. It was clear to me. Someone who was pierced for our transgressions. He was despised, et cetera. They were talking about Jesus. I told them that since I knew that it was Jesus they were speaking of, and Jesus wasn't in my Bible, the Old Testament, they had to be reading from the New Testament.

I wanted to make sure that, before I walked out, they knew that I wasn't offended, because I didn't want to offend them with my offense. But before I could get out the door, one of them asked me to wait a minute and sit back down. This wasn't the New Testament, he told me.

This was the Hebrew prophet, Isaiah. And as I sat down, he spun the Bible around so that I could read it for myself, and slid it in front of me. I was stunned at what I saw.

Right there in front of me, at the top of the page, in bold letters, was the name Isaiah. Good Jewish name. I knew of him. He was in my Bible. And there on the page, was what had just been read aloud, and more.

> "All of us like sheep have gone astray, each of us has turned to his own way; but the Lord has caused the iniquity of us all to fall on Him. He was oppressed and He was afflicted, yet He did not open His mouth; like a lamb that is led to slaughter, and like a sheep that is silent before its shearers, so He did not open His mouth. By oppression and judgment He was taken away; and as for His generation, who considered that He was cut off out of the land of the living for the transgression of my people, to whom the stroke was due? His grave was assigned with wicked men, yet He was with a rich man in His death, because He had done no violence, nor was there any deceit in His mouth. But the Lord was pleased to crush Him, putting Him to grief; if He would render Himself as a guilt offering, He will see His offspring, He will prolong His days, and the good pleasure of the Lord will prosper in His hand. As a result of the anguish of His soul, He will see it and be satisfied; by His knowledge the Righteous One, My Servant, will justify the many, as He will bear their iniquities. Therefore, I will allot Him a portion with the great, and He will divide the booty with the strong; because He poured out Himself to death, and was numbered with the transgressors; yet He Himself bore the sin of many, and interceded for the transgressors."
> (Isaiah 53:6-12 NASB)

Again, being the logical kind of person I was, there was no backing out. I had already told them I recognized that this passage was speaking of Jesus. Just because I had now been shown that what I had mistakenly believed to be the New Testament was, in fact, the Old Testament, didn't change my understanding of the passage. However, now I had a new problem.

My previous understanding that Jesus was not to be found in the Old Testament had been shattered. It was now clear to me that Jesus was to be found in my own Bible. But how should I process that information? While many will disagree with this process, the conclusions that I came to convinced me, beyond a shadow of a doubt, that Jesus was not just for my Gentile friends, but He was for me, and for everybody!

Isaiah was talking to my people. But He was talking to the Israelites on behalf of everyone. And not only was He for the Jewish people, He was from the Jewish people. He was one of us. And yet, as Isaiah noted, for the most part, we rejected Him. It wasn't supposed to be that way.

So now that I had a knowledge of who Jesus was, and that He was for me, I had no idea how to move forward. I was a part of the Jewish people, always had been, always would be, but the two—being Jewish and believing in Jesus—were to the best of my knowledge, incompatible. So for a long time, the knowledge of Christ remained dormant within me, along with the knowledge that I was the only Jewish person to ever come to the knowledge of Christ.

Ten years later, my wife-to-be Kim and I were looking for an officiant for our wedding. She came from both a Jewish and a Christian background. And we needed to find someone who would be acceptable to both the Jewish and the Christian members of the family. She came across a listing in the phone book called Messianic Judaism. And while neither of us were overly enthused with the idea, we both acknowledged that it would fulfill the requirements for both of our families.

It was several weeks before we were able to attend one of their services. It was strange right from the start, because they were meeting on Friday evenings, and they were calling their service a Shabbat service. It sounded Jewish enough, but it had been many years since I had been in a synagogue, and wasn't sure what to expect.

We were greeted by a couple that looked incredibly orthodox, which I was not accustomed to, but at least they were definitely recognizably Jewish. Kim and I went in and sat down. As the music began, there was an odd familiarity to it. The lyrics were mostly Hebrew, but that wasn't what struck me. It was the melodies.

There are some songs that just stick with you. And in the Jewish community, there are just some songs that everyone knows. I don't know how everyone comes to know them, we just do. A song like *Hava Nagila* is just born into you. We may not know the words, but we could hum along with the tune.

There was a song that I had been humming for years. I didn't know where I had picked it up, and I couldn't remember any of the words. Not a single one. But it was catchy. None of my friends knew it, so I thought that I might have imagined it, or could be remembering the tune incorrectly. And I wasn't trying to figure it out, nor was I going to try. But God had something prepared for me with this song.

As Kim and I were sitting listening to the music, something was stirring inside me. It was something Jewish, but there was something new. And then I heard it. That melody! I had thought that I would never figure it out, and had given up caring. But there it was! That was it! And there were words! "*Shalom rav, al Yisrael amcha, tasim l'olam*." Grant abundant peace upon Israel, your people, forever.

In that moment, I knew exactly what that peace was. It was the peace of Jesus. It was peace with a capital "P," and it was what I was feeling right then. It was the peace to know that it didn't matter what background I came from, it didn't matter that I was Jewish. Jesus, who I came to know as *Yeshua* - His Hebrew name – was for me. He always was. And here, in this small congregation, I learned that it was absolutely acceptable to be Jewish and believe.

The next thing I knew, I was crying. I didn't want my bride to see me, but I turned to look at her and, to my astonishment, she was crying, too! There was something that connected us, something that unified us that day. It connected us to each other, to the congregation, to believers everywhere, but also to the Jewishness that never made any sense until that day. Now it all came rushing back to me. It was all to equip me to worship the God of Abraham, Isaac, and Jacob, in spirit and in truth, by the power of His Son. And my life, and that of my bride, was changed forever.

I found it fascinating that, over the next weeks and months, which included a *mikveh*, a baptism by immersion, Kim and I had started living a more Jewish life. Not because we felt that we had to or some horrible curse was going to fall down upon us, but because we loved God in a new way, and felt that living that sort of life was a form of worship. Even more fascinating was the reaction from family and friends. For them, it wasn't our faith in Jesus that was problematic, because that was internal. No, it was the fact that we were beginning to look and act Jewish that was becoming an issue.

Today, when I think back on that time, I can only imagine what Paul must have been feeling when he wrote about his broken heart for his people, Israel. I remember making a promise to God that day in the congregation that had two parts. The first part was that if there was any way I could help to share the peace of Jesus with my Jewish brothers and sisters, I would do it. And the second part was that if there was any way I could help those Jewish brothers and sisters who found the Lord to find a place to worship and still be Jewish, I would do it. The only problem was that I didn't really take into consideration that God was listening. He answered me and took me at my word.

Today, by God's grace, Kim and I have the privilege of being emissaries on behalf of Yeshua to the Jewish people with Chosen People Ministries, in fulfillment of the first part of that promise. I am also the rabbi of *Kehilat Sar Shalom*, which means the Congregation of the Prince of Peace, which is the fulfillment of the second part. We have both come a long way from the twenty-somethings that walked into that congregation many years ago. And yet, there is still such a long way to go.

I truly believe in my heart that Jesus is the light of the world, given to the world – yes, that means to everyone – by a God who loves His creation. He is the great connector, binding all those who believe together, in love. And yet, because He is the light of the world, He has this unique ability to bind us all together, to transcend earthly beliefs and desires, and transform us into something greater. He did it in Ephesians when He took the Jew and the Gentile and told them both that it was not acceptable to despise something that He had already made clean, thus uniting them together. This was a feat that neither would have said was possible up to that point.

God still has that power to do so. But we have to have the faith that He can do it. He promised that He would. Abraham, who was not only the father of the Jewish people, but the role model for ALL people of faith, believed that He would keep His promise. And it was that belief for which God gave him credit as righteousness. And it is only through that kind of faith that we will ever attain *tikkun olam*, the restoration of the world. And the only way to reach that kind of unity is through Yeshua, Jesus, the light of the world.

Neal Surasky was raised in a traditional Jewish home. He first heard about the Messiah during his senior year in high school, but it wasn't until years later that he accepted Yeshua (Jesus) into his life. He met and fell in love with his wife, Kim, at the end of his tour of duty in the U.S. Army. During the planning for their wedding, they were both introduced to Messianic Judaism, and they began their walk with the Lord together.

Neal and Kim joined the staff of Chosen People Ministries in 2006, and in 2007, Neal was inaugurated as the Rabbi of Kehilat Sar Shalom, (Congregation of the Prince of Peace) in northern Virginia. He was promoted to the position of Washington, DC Branch Director in 2010, and continues working toward his Master of Divinity degree at the Feinberg Center for Messianic Jewish Studies. Neal and Kim have 5 children—2 girls and 3 boys— and 4 grandchildren, all boys.

NEVER LOSE HOPE
Chester Mitchell

"Hope is the word, which God has written on the brow of every man." — Victor Hugo

It was a crisp New York morning. The leaves were just beginning to fall on New York's Long Island. That morning, September 30, 2012, a petite-framed woman, along with six tall men, took the elevator from the ground floor of the hospital to the intensive care unit.

They entered the unit and marched single file into the room. Lying in the bed was a man of 89 years. A few days earlier, he had arrived home from the same hospital.

He had been struggling to breathe when he made the seventh and last step that led up to his home on Lakeview Avenue. At that moment, he realized that he needed to rest…. but he collapsed with a massive heart attack.

By all accounts, he died on the steps of his home. This was his final wish, "to go home." Twenty minutes later he arrived again at Long Island's Mercy Hospital and, through the heroic efforts of the doctors and nurses, a faint pulse was found. He was connected to a respirator, which allowed him to keep breathing until his family could decide when to release him "*to go home.*"

The day had arrived and Myrtle Mitchell, along with her six sons, was there to witness something that we never thought would happen… the death of my dad.

For over an hour we sang hymns and prayed over Dad. The doctor came and essentially told us what we already knew. Dad's vital organs had begun to shut down. I wanted to know how long he would live without the help of the machines. The good doctor sidestepped the question with a general answer, which was code for, *"I don't know, but I think it will not be long."*

Once the machine was disconnected, we began singing the familiar hymn, *Great Is Thy Faithfulness.*

I shall never forget standing next to Mom as she stood next to my father. Dad was now taking one shallow breath after another. Somewhere in my mind, I could hear the words, *"Just one more breath!"* Dad breathed for about 15 minutes and then I watched as he took several short ones…. and then he took his last. Fifteen minutes of breathing and my dad was in heaven.

In spite of our tears, we had no doubt that Dad had arrived safely home. How can I be sure? When I am sure about what God has done, I can be confident about what is to come.

To appreciate the moment of my dad's passing, you have to hear the rest of the story.

———

Her name was Myrtle Braham. She was the only daughter of Winnifred and Arnold. "Master Arnold" is what the locals in Robins Bay and the surrounding communities called him. He was short, well built, and he had what seemed to me the most piercing eyes. He was the District Constable. He was the local lawman—sheriff, if you please. Whenever someone needed to be arrested, Arnold Braham did it.

We called her "Miss Winnie." She had eyes that twinkled. She was petite—fragile. But she was strong and resilient. My grandparents were my heroes.

Each summer, my brothers and I would pile into my dad's car and make the two-hour drive from Kingston to the Parish of St. Mary on the beautiful island of Jamaica. We lived for the months that we spent with our grandparents.

The road from Kingston was paved—until we were almost to Robins Bay. The last two miles, the road turned gravel. Potholes abounded from the tide of the nearby Caribbean Sea. Robins Bay was the place that time had forgotten…but not God.

The year was 1947. Sutliff Logan was a local in Robin's Bay by the sea. That year, he left home to join with a group of men who had been hired to work on farms in the state of Ohio. Little did he know that God had a greater purpose for his life.

While in Ohio, Sutliff Logan heard the message of the Gospel. He placed his faith in Christ and became a believer. Shortly after, he returned home to Jamaica. Logan became a pastor and built a humble church.

The structure was made of bamboo and the floor was covered with sawdust. It was here that my mom came to faith in Christ. Pastor "Sut" baptized her in the ocean and grace altered the trajectory of her life. But there was a greater story still.

Years later, my mom moved to the capital city of Kingston where she met Alfred Mitchell. They married and she gave birth to seven sons. During most of my life, my dad was not a Christian. While he was a good father and husband, it seemed as if he was never going to surrender his life to the Lordship of Christ.

What I remember most about my mother was her fierce commitment to Christ and her unrelenting prayer for the salvation of my father and her boys. Quite often we pray prayers that are answered immediately. But some prayers take time—a very long time. The prayer for my dad would take almost fifty years before it was answered.

I still remember my mother taking the bus to church, Sunday after Sunday, with her boys. Later in New York, we would take the bus and the train to church. I remember the wonderful people in our church asking my mom if Dad had given his life to Christ. After a while, I grew somewhat embarrassed, each time the question was asked. Not so with Mom. She would answer with a calm resolve, "Not yet."

After college I moved to California to train for ministry. Sixteen years later, I arrived in Ashburn, Virginia to plant the church I now pastor, Capital Community Church.

Shortly after settling in Virginia, I travelled to New York. My brother, Mike, had completed the building of the church he pastors in Brooklyn. That weekend after the message by our friend Pastor Jack Cunningham, I looked over at my dad. This was one of the rare times that he attended a church gathering. In that moment, I prayed a silent, simple prayer. "God, please save my dad." With that prayer completed, I stepped off the stage, walked over to my dad, and led him to Christ.

That day will always live in my heart as a reminder that: 1. God's love reaches farther than we often think. 2. God never forgets the prayers that are sometimes forgotten by the people who spoke them. 3. No matter how long you have been praying…. just keep on praying.

The September morning that we gathered around my dad's hospital bed was bittersweet. Bitter...because Dad would no longer be with us in human form. Just a few breaths away from heaven. Sweet...because God still travels down gravel roads to find one person who has the faith to believe for what seems impossible.

Chester Mitchell is the lead pastor of Capital Community Church in Ashburn Virginia, which he and his wife founded in 1996. For almost thirty years, Pastor Mitchell has used his gifts as a communicator, leadership coach and mentor to impart God's grace and to motivate people to reach their highest potential. He is the author of two books, The Gravel Road to Heaven *and* The Healing Road to Heaven. *He has been happily married to his best friend, Marion, for 29 years. They live in Ashburn, Virginia. He blogs at www.chestermitchell.org.*

THE GREATEST GIFT
Holly Calhoun Leachman

My name is Holly Calhoun Leachman, and this is my story. For so many years, I was lost, unable to find my way, but God lovingly led me to a place where I was found, loved, and secure!

I was born at Piedmont Hospital in Atlanta, Georgia. My parents had prayed for two boys and two girls, and God granted them exactly that! With four kids spanning five years, each of our births served as a stepping-stone to an increasingly full and crazy household. Adding to the mix, two dachshund puppies named Otto and Missy protected us, played with us, and added to the delight of a precious childhood in the South.

A picturesque neighborhood set the stage for our childhood, full of grand pine, oak, maple and dogwood trees. We climbed the maples, built tree houses in the pines, and threw many a pinecone from high above at innocent passersby. The fun extended beyond our family to the whole neighborhood. For example, we had Easter egg hunts, with a gaggle of kids running around with baskets in hand and searching for those timeless colored plastic eggs holding candy and toy treasures. On the 4th of July, the scene was pure Americana, with fireworks, sparklers, hamburgers, and hot dogs. And flags. Lots of flags.

Thanksgiving meant a road trip, with all six of us piling into our station wagon, and Mom and Dad quite literally driving us over the river and through the woods to Macon, Georgia, to the home of our granddad and Aunt Martha. The menu was complete with turkey and dressing, sweet potato casserole with marshmallows, brown sugar and pecans, string beans, corn, cranberry sauce, mashed potatoes with gravy, and homemade rolls that would melt in your mouth – a grand feast, indeed! The challenge was to eat everything in sight while saving some room for pie. We Southerners are serious about our pies. Those pies were legendary, beautiful to see, delicious to eat! Aunt Martha baked an array of pies: peach, pumpkin, apple or cherry. Pecan pie was my favorite, but I always indulged in some pumpkin, too, for the sake of Thanksgiving tradition.

Christmas was another memorable time with plays at school, pageants at church, and relatives crowding into our home, with the result being lots of food, presents, and chaos! Naturally, when the New Year finally arrived, we four kids would head back to school, as our parents exhaled a sigh of relief. Appropriately, we all attended our neighborhood public school, Margaret Mitchell Elementary School, named after the author of *Gone with the Wind*. Subsequently, we went to Lovett, a private school highly regarded for its academic record and excellent teachers. I earned good grades, had many friends, played sports, went to church regularly, and sang in the choir. My whole family had been baptized and confirmed. My dad was a respected lawyer, my mom a popular teacher. What could possibly go wrong?

What went wrong with me is what goes wrong with most people. I went my own way. My great desire was to please others, to be popular, to have fun. I thought these motivations were harmless. But where did that lead me?

I found myself on a destructive path. Pleasing others meant I compromised continually, and my priority became simply to do what my friends wanted, whether or not in direct conflict to how I had been raised.

I first rebelled by smoking cigarettes in hidden places with friends or neighbors. We formed a secret "Bamboo Club" for this very purpose. We literally met in a dense area of bamboo to smoke, the cigarettes often stolen from someone's parents' supply. Despite my idyllic childhood, the downward spiral began.

Sounds crazy, doesn't it? But the momentum of the spiral is hard to stop. One lie leads to another, dishonesty breeds mistrust, guilt and shame set in, and a heart turns dark. So subtle are these changes initially, we hardly notice it ourselves.

I didn't see it. I was too busy pleasing others. I was the good party girl. I drank a lot. I took great pride in the fact that I could drink many guys under the table. While I could drink many a beer, I actually pitied the girls that couldn't hold their liquor! My life seemed to be going very well. With good grades, plenty of dates and parties to attend, I lived a seemingly ideal life as a cheerleader, belonging to clubs and high school sororities. Surely this was the high life.

But when I let myself be quiet, I knew something was missing. No one else could see it. But I knew something was not right. It was me. I was lost.

Webster's Dictionary defines lost as "not being in the designed or designated place." I was not where I was designed to be. I know

now that we are all designed to be close to our Lord, in a transforming relationship with our Creator God. But at 17 years old, I was looking for love "in all the wrong places." And in this search for love, the Lord got my attention. In English class, we had to memorize I Corinthians 13:1-13. I was familiar with this beautiful passage, but I had no idea what power these words would have in my young life.

> "If I speak with the tongues of men and angels and have not love, I am only a resounding gong or a clanging cymbal. If I have the gift of prophecy and can fathom all mysteries and all knowledge, and if I have a faith that can move mountains, but have not love, I am nothing. If I give all I possess to the poor and surrender my body to the flames, but have not love I gain nothing. Love is patient, love is kind, love is not jealous, it does not boast, it is not proud. It is not rude, it is not self-seeking, it is not easily angered, it keeps no record of wrongs. Love does not delight in evil but rejoices with the truth. It always protects, always trust, always hopes, always perseveres. Love never fails. But where there are prophecies, they will cease; where there are tongues, they will be stilled; where there is knowledge, it will pass away. For we know in part and we prophesy in part, but when perfection comes, the imperfect disappears. When I was a child, I talked like a child, I thought like a child, I reasoned like a child. When I became a man, I put childish ways behind me. Now we see but a poor reflection as in a mirror; then we shall see face to face. Now I know in part; then I shall know fully, even as I am fully known. And now these three remain: faith, hope and love. But the greatest of these is love." (NIV)

How amazing were these life-giving words to me! At 17 years old, I was constantly infatuated with someone. I was certain that my version of love was real and true. Then I would recite those powerful words that I had learned…"Love is patient, love is kind, love is not jealous"....... *Not jealous? How could that possibly be true?* I thought I was in love, yet I was always gripped by jealousy.

I had two options: this proclamation of true love from God's word could either crush me or rescue me. I started to look at myself in a different light, examining the contradictions within myself. *How could I be "in love" and so jealous at the same time? Where could I ever find this real love – this true love that was patient and kind, not jealous or haughty or rude?*

I began searching, asking my teachers, my friends, my priest, where was this love to be found? No one had an answer.

I prayed about it. I asked the Lord to help me find this kind of love. A friend invited me to a Young Life club meeting. I didn't know anything about Young Life, but out of regard for my friend, I visited. I learned that Young Life was a nondenominational Christian organization that reached out to high school kids with the love of Jesus Christ. Young Life clubs met (and still do!) in local homes, in gatherings that included snacks, songs, skits, and a short message from the Bible. I was intrigued. I questioned, I listened.

Through all that, I began to see. God's presence was becoming increasingly clear to me. The God that I had earlier learned so much about at home and church was real!

I had been raised with prayers at the dinner table, prayers at bedtime. At church I sang the hymns, heard the sermons, recited the proper prayers. I knew that Jesus was born in a manger, and that shepherds, angels, and wise men from afar all came to see him. I knew that Jesus died on a cross and rose from the dead. I knew all these details about the life of Jesus, but I did not know Him. I had head knowledge but lacked heart knowledge.

Young Life operates by the motto: "Every kid deserves a chance to hear the gospel in a language he can understand." Because of Young Life leaders who lived this out, I finally heard the Gospel with my heart. These young men and women loved us and taught us about the life and teachings of Jesus Christ.

I had heard many of these teachings earlier on, but now I started hearing the message and this good news about Jesus Christ with amazing clarity. What was happening? Was God really answering me?

After memorizing 1 Corinthian 13, I remember telling God, *"If this kind of love really exists, then I do not want to live my whole life and never have it!"*

If this kind of love was possible, I wanted it. Where was it? I continued my search. I wondered how I could ever find the person who would love me with this kind of love. How could I interview one million men to find him?

December of my senior year of high school, I went on a Young Life cruise with hundreds of other kids from Atlanta. We hopped on buses to Miami where we boarded a cruise ship for Nassau. What an adventure! Tons of fun, crazy games, hysterical skits. No drugs, no alcohol, just great fun.

So where was this I Corinthians 13 love? I saw evidences of it all around me.

But where was it for me? One night, the Young Life leader told the story of the cross. I thought I knew this story pretty well. But this time was different, this time it was personal. Jesus Christ, the Son of GOD, died for me, a 17-year-old sinner. Wow! That is incredible! I prayed and asked the Lord to come into my heart and live in me. I thanked Him for dying on the cross for me and for my sins. I asked the Lord what He wanted, and in my heart I sensed that He just wanted me. "Well, Lord, you can have me," was my simple, sincere reply. That was the answer to all my questions. Here was that great love! Love that was patient and kind, love that was not haughty or jealous or rude. God was the source all the time. He demonstrated this awesome love to me and to the world through Jesus Christ. Finally, everything made sense. I really could know this love, receive this love, and give this love to others. What a great gift! The words of the old hymn now applied to me: "Amazing grace, how sweet the sound that saved a wretch like me. I once was lost, but now I'm found, was blind but now I see."

I experienced an amazing transformation. I was a new person. I found I Corinthians 5:17-19, to be true: "Therefore, if anyone is in Christ, he is a new creation; the old has gone, the new has come. All this is from God, who reconciled us to Himself through Christ and gave us the ministry of reconciliation: that God was reconciling the world to Himself in Christ, not counting men's sins against them." (NIV)

This is great news for a 17-year-old or a 97-year-old! I had a chance to be new, to have a clean slate! My wrongs, my sins, my foolishness, were not counted against me! Jesus Christ paid my debt in full. That is truly outrageous!

So the new me made some changes. I stopped drinking. It wasn't hard. It was simply the right thing to do. My friends teased me, some mocked me, others snubbed me, but I didn't care. I was a new person and confident in my new identity. I was really loved, personally, totally, completely. The love portrayed by I Corinthians 13 really did exist and now I had it. God answered my prayers!

Through the years, I have faced many challenges, and many joys and sorrows. The year after I gave my heart to the Lord, my dear dad died of cancer. The Lord was my comfort and strength. I had never known such a great sorrow. I learned that the Lord promised to be a Father to the fatherless. What great love is this that God Himself would provide for me in such a tender way.

When I left for college that year, I simply took my Father's love with me. When grades came out, I took the paper to the little chapel on campus and showed my heavenly Father what I had achieved. I wasn't sure how all this worked, but if God was a personal Father to the fatherless, then that included me and I was going to act accordingly.

The personal love of God found in Jesus Christ has totally changed my life. I never have to face anything alone. The Lord has promised to never leave me or forsake me. This great adventure started 44 years ago and I am still learning and growing in Him who loves me.

The greatest gift I have ever received is this gift of true love, real forgiveness, and a new life found in Jesus Christ.

Holly Calhoun Leachman was born and raised in Atlanta, GA. For the last 30 years, she has called the DC area her home. She and her husband, Jerry, have been married for over 40 years. They have 3 grown children and 5 grandchildren.

She enjoys fun times with family & friends, studying and teaching God's Word, hiking in Colorado, walking on beaches, visiting gardens, gardening, and watching SEC football games. You can learn more about Holly at LeachmanMinistries.org.

OUR JOURNEY OF FAITH

Isaac Huang

My ancestors moved from Fujian Province in China to settle in Taiwan in the 18th century. We spoke the Southern Fujian dialect. My great grandfather on my father's side was a scholar in the final years of the Qing Dynasty (1644-1912) and because of this, education has been the heritage of our family generation after generation. All our males were educated in Confucian thinking and were quite proud of this tradition.

In the Sino-Japanese War of 1895, China was defeated by Japan. Taiwan became a Japanese colony for 50 years. The Taiwanese people were required to learn to speak Japanese and accept Japanese education. In 1945, Japan was defeated in WWII; Taiwan was returned to China and once again the Taiwanese people learned Mandarin, China's national language.

My parents and grandparents, therefore, grew up in an era in which the victors of war defined and redefined Taiwan's culture. But the chaos of this period did not prevent God's servants from coming to Taiwan with the good news of salvation through Jesus Christ. Among these church planters were medical doctors James Maxwell of Scotland, who came in 1864, and George Mackay of Canada, who arrived in 1871. Unfortunately, during the period of Japanese occupation, many churches were closed because they refused to recognize the Japanese emperor as a god, and many pastors were imprisoned. After WWII, missionaries came once again from Europe and North America.

As memory serves, my maternal grandmother was the first on both sides of the family to believe in Jesus. When I was child, she told me that around 1950 a Scottish missionary led her to the Lord. Later, she lost contact with him. After a number of years, she took me to a Christian gathering and unexpectedly ran into this missionary again, which brought her great joy. What really surprised me was that this missionary used my mother tongue of Southern Fujian dialect to speak with my grandma. He spoke very accurately, as well as any Taiwanese would. This was the first time that I was moved by the passion of an ambassador of Christ.

My grandmother helped both my parents trust in Jesus for salvation. My mother came to belief in Jesus in the early 1950s, shortly before marrying my father. He was not a Christian, but agreed to hold their wedding ceremony in a church. Both my grandmother and the pastor who conducted my parents' wedding ceremony enthusiastically introduced Jesus to my father. Based on my father's own description, he felt, arrogantly, that abandoning the traditions of his own culture to follow Jesus was an act of weakness. For three years, he debated with the pastor on his need for God. That faithful servant of God responded in patience and much prayer. Setbacks in my father's clothing design and manufacturing business forced him to thoroughly recognize his own weakness and limitations. It got to the point that he was going to sell wares on a blanket by the side of the road to survive. He finally responded to the Holy Spirit's conviction by choosing to trust his life and salvation solely to the Jesus he had despised.

After my father's step of faith, he restarted the business, this time following Biblical principles for its operation. He hired Christians as his senior staff and established a "Workers Fellowship," through which both believing and seeking employees could benefit from Bible teaching. The company would stop work on Monday mornings to hold fellowship meetings. Some people were afraid that this would result in losses for the company, but instead God blessed his obedience and caused his business to flourish. In a mostly pagan environment, this was a powerful story, and his company became a model for others led by Christians. Most important, many people trusted in Jesus as a result of his initiative.

God also blessed my father's service in his church as he assisted the pastor. God led the church to reach out to Taiwanese aborigines. These are people who share genes and language with about 400 million "Austronesian" people across Southeast Asia and the South Pacific. My father's church planted ten churches among the aborigines in the mountain areas of Taiwan, and he played an important role in this missionary work.

During this time, my father's heart was heavy because his mother had still not believed in Jesus. Generally, Chinese families have a tradition that parents go to live with their eldest son when they become old. Although my father was the third son, his mother preferred staying with him. He told her that she could live with us, but that Christians do not set out any idols or memorial tablets for ancestors in our homes. She agreed to abide by this restriction. Even though my parents often shared the Gospel with my grandma, she was also influenced by other relatives who would take her to the local Buddhist temple.

My father's love eventually moved her, however, to attend church services with us, albeit a bit reluctantly. Our other relatives responded by stirring up dissension between my mother and grandmother. The unfortunate effect was tension between my parents, as my father was torn between the two women he loved most. Stress between mother- and daughter-in-law is not uncommon in Chinese families, but for a newly established Christian family, it was truly a challenge.

When my grandmother was 81, she contracted a severe case of pneumonia that almost took her life. While she was sick, superstitious relatives went to the temple to consult idols. An evil spirit influenced a medium to tell these relatives that the reason Grandma had contracted a serious illness was that her going to church offended our deceased grandfather. Grandpa therefore wanted to pull her down into the netherworld. The demon emphasized that if my parents had not taken Grandma to church she would not have become sick.

When my father heard this accusation, he prayed and informed the church. My father was a devoted and obedient son who resolutely believed that God would heal my grandmother and give her the opportunity to believe in Jesus. During the two days she was in critical condition, the church urgently prayed, and God answered with healing. Grandma's illness suddenly took a turn for the better and she was soon able to leave the hospital.

After she had fully recovered, she told my father that she was willing to believe in Jesus and wanted to be baptized as a testimony of what Jesus had done for her. My father was elated, and invited the pastor and church elders to hear her story. Grandma told the pastor that a person wearing white shining clothes came to her bedside and said, "Madame, don't worry, I will heal your illness and let you live for many years." Great peace and joy became evident in my grandmother's life. She eagerly told our relatives what the Lord had done for her.

Amazingly, when those superstitious relatives went to the temple again to consult with the idols, the evil spirit told them this time not to ask again about Grandma, since "she is no longer under my jurisdiction." Through this experience and the testimonies of my parents and grandmother, many members of our extended family put their trust in Jesus. On the day after my grandmother's 100th birthday, she went to be with her Savior and Lord.

Although Christians, our family was far from perfect. My parents continued to quarrel, to the point that they eventually lived separately; my mother took my younger brother and sister to live in another city. I was in high school and remained with my father. His business was all-consuming, and his parenting style was harsh. I struggled psychologically, and was bitter and unforgiving toward him. Although I was steeped in church practices and beliefs, our family situation made me feel that, even if God existed, He was probably far from me. I certainly did not have a relationship with Him.

When I moved away for college, I stopped going to church and wandered for two years. During this period, God used the emptiness of my heart and the wounds I had received from my family to compel me to earnestly think about the meaning of man's existence. I tried other religions and philosophies, but failed to find satisfactory answers.

By my third year of university, I despaired and came to the point of wondering why I should continue living. But a voice in my heart said, "Why not take a look at the Bible that you read as a child? Maybe you will find an answer there." So when someone invited me to a meeting of the Campus Evangelical Fellowship, I went. I sensed an invitation from Jesus to follow Him through the messages of the speakers. I began attending a student-led small group, and started to reconsider my relationship with God. With the little faith I had, I started to pray for my family and myself, seeking God's healing. Later I became aware that my father was also praying in the same way. God heard our prayers and, through a letter exchange, I reconciled with my father. Afterward, my father courageously took the step of admitting his mistakes to my mother and all the children, asking for their forgiveness. My father's humility saved our family from falling to pieces.

Late one night, as I read the Bible, God used John 3:16-18 to convict my heart, allowing me to see that I was a sinner and that I would be lost forever when I left the world if my sins were not resolved. God loved me so much that He sent His own Son to pay the penalty for my sins with His blood. By raising Jesus from the dead, God proved His power over death itself. In order to live eternally, I had to put my trust in Jesus, and Jesus alone.

God reminded me of the stories of my parents and grandmothers. I remembered how enthusiastic the people who shared the Gospel with them were, and I thought about all of the Christians that God had brought into my life. I thanked God for hearing my prayers and miraculously changing my father's heart. It suddenly became clear to me that God had been calling me all along and taking care of me. God hadn't been far from me; I was far from Him! I kneeled in tears, acknowledged my sin, repented, and believed that Jesus was my Savior and Lord. I felt the Lord embracing me and welcoming me back home. I had finally found the answer. This universe has a God who created us. He loves us and, while we were still in sin, His love led Him to come into the world to save us. Only when we are willing to put our trust in Him does our existence have meaning. I was soon baptized as a testimony that I had been saved and become a child of God.

I thank the Lord that my life was forever changed. He brought me into a life I could have never imagined. I've experienced joy of fellowship with other believers and a love for people that compels me to tell others what Jesus wants to do for them. God continues to help me grow in maturity through the Bible, the work of His spirit, and His church. He's also given me a godly wife to walk with me in this life devoted to God, and to build a Christ-centered family.

In 1982, God led my wife and me to study at Old Dominion University's graduate school in Norfolk, Virginia. That gave us the opportunity to live and work with North American Christians. Upon graduation in 1984, a job opportunity moved us to Northern Virginia near Washington, DC.

During our first few years here, we were part of churches that primarily spoke Mandarin and our Southern Fujian dialect. God equipped us there for His next step. To integrate more into American society and in consideration of the spiritual needs of our son and daughter, we became part of Chantilly Bible Church, a mainly English-speaking church. There was something special about this church. It was particularly welcoming to immigrants. Several years earlier, a handful of Chinese believers began meeting in the church for Bible study. Their numbers grew, and the CBC elders invited them to become part of the church, bringing in an English-speaking former missionary to Asia to pastor the new "Chinese congregation." Interpreters ensured that the immigrants benefited from hearing sermons in both English and their heart language of Mandarin.

After we came to the church in 1996, my role gradually increased as God and the church elders entrusted more responsibilities to me. Eventually, I began to sense that God was calling me to serve Him full-time. After careful prayer, I responded in obedience to the call. In 2000, I left my information technology career and entered seminary for Bible training. Upon graduation, I assumed pastoral responsibility for CBC's Chinese ministries, a privilege and joy that continues today. Between the first Mandarin worship service in 1992 and the summer of 2011, the Chinese component of Chantilly Bible Church grew from 30 people to over 600.

Northern Virginia is home to people from around the world, and our church has embraced this diversity. In addition to our large Chinese population, we have smaller Hispanic, Indian, and Korean groups of believers who want to be part of what God is doing in and through CBC. God led the elders of the church to gradually understand His intent. At CBC, God wants people from different cultures and languages to attain and preserve unity in Christ, as a single local church of many nations. Together we can accomplish our mission of "making disciples of Christ who are winning, growing, and serving" in our multi-cultural community.

One result of this understanding of God's will for CBC was the elimination, in the fall of 2011, of the Sunday morning Chinese worship service, in favor of services that combine all of our ethnic groups. During these services, English is the primary language, but we provide simultaneous interpretation via headsets for our Mandarin and Spanish speakers, plus written translation of the sermon in Chinese to help people follow along. We maintain many smaller groups and venues for people to enjoy their affinities, be they culture, language, interest, age, or gender. But on Sunday mornings, we are one church, meeting all together to worship our Lord.

God is teaching us to forbear, accept, and reconcile with one another in Christ. Our common bond in Christ enables us to grow, serve, and celebrate together. God has expanded my ministry through this transformation, and I now have responsibilities that involve working with groups in our church other than Chinese. Everyone on our staff encourages our church family to embrace our cultural diversity even when it means moving out of our comfort zones. Doing this requires conforming to the love of Christ, obeying God's Word through the power of the Holy Spirit, making intentional efforts, and maintaining a prayerful heart.

From what we can tell in observing other churches, we are on a unique journey. Our trust is in God and we find great encouragement in the Apostle Paul's words, "For I am confident of this very thing, that He who began a good work in you will perfect it until the day of Jesus Christ."

As I look back at what God has done for me, my family and His church, I see clearly that He is full of love, truth, and faithfulness. If we are willing to trust Him with our life journey, God will make us more like Jesus and use us for His good purposes. May all glory be to Him, now and forever!

Isaac Huang grew up in Taiwan, where he put his trust in the Lord during his junior year of college. Isaac and his wife, Ramona, moved to the U.S. in 1982 for graduate study in engineering. Isaac was working as a computer programmer when he and Ramona visited Capital Bible Seminary of Lanham, MD in 1996. They were deeply moved by CBC's sound biblical teaching and sincere welcome to immigrants.

Years of volunteer service led Isaac to leave his high-tech job to obtain a Master's in Christian Counseling and Discipleship from Capital Bible Seminary. Isaac has served as pastor of Chinese Ministries since 2002. He has a heart to reach immigrants, particularly professionals. Isaac and Ramona have two children, Jonathan and Joyce. Isaac enjoys listening to classical music, cooking and spending time with people.

Also available from Believe Books:

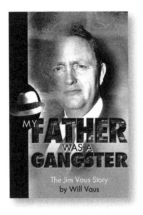

Will Vaus

MY FATHER WAS A GANGSTER
The Jim Vaus Story

One of the most fascinating conversion stories of the 20th century—the dramatic life story of Jim Vaus, former associate to America's underworld.

Terri Whitaker

YESUPADAM
Reaching India's Untouched

Yesupadam is the amazing story of God's miraculous work through an Untouchable Indian believer in Jesus and his Love-n-Care ministry in eastern India.

Fanny Goose
with Janet Fridman

RISING FROM THE HOLOCAUST
The Life of Fanny Goose

The astonishing real life story of an indomitable young Jewish girl who miraculously survives the horrors of Hitler's plot to destroy her people and goes on to live a joyful life.

Also available from Believe Books:

Major General Jerry R. Curry

FROM PRIVATE TO GENERAL
An African American Soldier Rises Through the Ranks

Major General Jerry Curry vividly describes his life journey of military missions, powerful positions, and his relationship with the true source of authority—his Father in heaven.

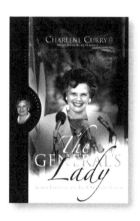

Charlene Curry

THE GENERAL'S LADY
God's Faithfulness to a Military Spouse

Charlene Curry recounts all the joys and challenges of being a career military spouse and how she triumphed over difficulties by relying on a source of spiritual power that transformed her life.

Fern C. Willner

WHEN FAITH IS ENOUGH
A Safari of Destiny that Reveals Principles to Live By

A faith-inspiring story of a missionary wife and mother of seven relying completely on God in the heart of Africa.

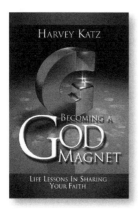

Harvey Katz

BECOMING A GOD MAGNET
The Secret to Sharing Your Faith
Book and Study & Discussion Guide

Harvey Katz's book *Becoming a God Magnet* is a practical, effective guide to evangelism. The Study & Discussion Guide is ideal for church or home groups willing to learn and share successful methods of personal evangelism.

Howard Katz

SEVEN ESSENTIAL RELATIONSHIPS
How To Pass God's Crucial Tests

The author uses the seven stages in the creation of a clay vessel, as well as an exposition of the life of Joseph, to illustrate each of the seven crucial tests that every believer must pass.

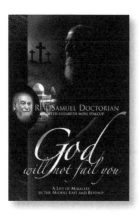

Rev. Samuel Doctorian
with Elizabeth Moll Stalcup, Ph.D.

GOD WILL NOT FAIL YOU
A Life of Miracles in the Middle East and Beyond

The miraculous life story of Rev. Samuel Doctorian, the renowned evangelist used mightily by God in the Middle East and around the world.

Also available from Believe Books:

Mary Haskett

REVEREND MOTHER'S DAUGHTER
A Real Life Story

In this gripping account, the author shares her personal story of racial rejection, physical and sexual abuse, and wartime trauma. Through it all, she is aware of a driving force in her life that ultimately brings her to Jesus Christ.

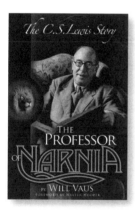

Will Vaus

THE PROFESSOR OF NARNIA –
The C.S. Lewis Story

This unique telling of the life story of C.S. Lewis, which interweaves the writing of each of his books with the unfolding of his own personal journey of faith, is a favorite with home-schoolers, book clubs, and Christian schools, as well as with all fans of *The Chronicles of Narnia.*

Donna Goodrich

HEALING IN GOD'S TIME
Trusting in God's Faithfulness on the Journey to a Miracle

When award-winning gospel music songwriter Dave Clark awoke one morning with what he thought was a sore throat, little did he or his family suspect that it was the beginning of a 19-year battle with a painful disease. Read this wonderful story about the faithfulness of God that keeps Dave disease-free today, enabling him to write music to help others who are hurting.

---

www.BelieveBooks.com

Brenwyd Legacy Trilogy *by Rosemary Groux*

BOOK 1: FINDING TRUTH

Finding Truth is the tale of Cassie Pennington, a teenage girl on an epic quest to rescue her kidnapped parents and discover the truth about her own identity and destiny. Her life takes a turn for the adventurous when she learns that she is descended from the Brenwyds, an ancient group of people who are as much in danger as they are gifted.

BOOK 2: FINDING SECRETS

In *Finding Secrets,* Cassie and her friends journey to Glastonbury, where they meet a mysterious woman who holds the key to their past – and their future. Suddenly thrust through a musical "time slip," the teens find themselves in a kingdom ruled by none other than the legendary King Arthur. Before they can return and finish the rescue mission they began in their own era, the four friends discover that they have a vital role to play in this one.

BOOK 3: FINDING FREEDOM

An epic battle ensues in *Finding Freedom*, going beyond the physical, with spiritual forces at work on both sides. Much is at stake: the vast treasure hoard of King Arthur, the personal safety of Cassie and those she holds dear, and the future of all Brenwyds. Cassie has not forgotten the prophecy foretelling her role in the conflict and wonders if she can live up to such an extraordinary destiny.